# Sweet Seasons of Miracles

### Stories of Encouragement and Hope in Times of Trial

By  Jewels Mesaros

ISBN Number: 1-4276-0980-2

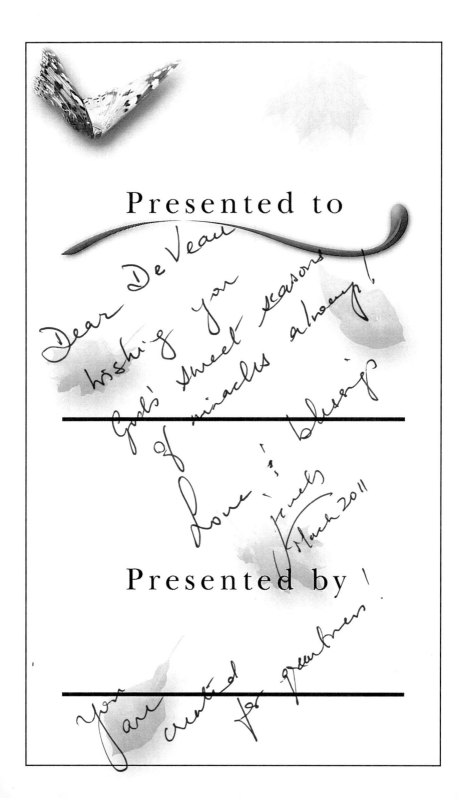

## Presented to

Dear DeVeau,
Wishing you
God's sweet seasons
of miracles always!

Love & blessings,

[signature]
March 2011

## Presented by

Your
Aunt
created for greatness.

# Dedication

Pete – My husband and miracle without whose
encouragement this book would not have been possible.

Venus and Neptune – My two precious daughters
who walked through life's trials and watched
these miracles unfold.


Above all
Dedicated To My God - *The Great Miracle Worker*

*Dear Reader,*

Have you ever found yourself in a despairing and hopeless situation with no way out?

***Sweet Seasons of Miracles*** brings to you stories of encouragement and hope in times of trial.

You will find a sense of expectancy and hope that comes like a shaft of light in the midst of very challenging times as you journey through this book across the continents. The stories have a near universal appeal to anyone wanting to travel without having to really leave the comfort of their home or hearth.

In this book you get a glimpse into the plight and woes of street children in India and how our love and involvement can make a difference. It is my belief that no one should have to live this way, least among them, children.

***Sweet Seasons of Miracles*** is an account of God's faithfulness bringing love, wrapped in human endeavors.

Writing these stories and assembling them have been an important part of my life. I share these stories to bring that one thing that we all look for "hope".

As you read this book you will be encouraged to believe in the impossible and find that what might seem to be an expected and boring end can get turned around into an unexpected life changing miracle.

This book is a way for me to thank God for the sweet seasons of miracles in my own life.

*Jewels Mesaros*

# Table of Contents

# Chapter - 1

## The Miracle of a Safe Landing

Even as a child, I always wanted to travel. I lived in a little house with my parents and two brothers in the heart of the city of Bombay, India.

Home to me was a cross between a secret garden in the midst of a lush green village and a humming township in a city that was the commercial capital of India.

While other girls my age were playing with dolls, I would clamber up a giant mango tree, look toward the horizon and dream of other lands and other people. I loved to read, and stories from distant lands fascinated and inspired me.

By the time I was eighteen I was consumed with the idea of hitchhiking through India and someday, the whole world.

My mother's good sense kept me from doing something as dangerous as hitchhiking at eighteen but that did not keep me from flying on wings of imagination, every so often, into distant lands.

Now in my thirties I was actually flying to Europe.

I had been invited by a church to come and speak about what God was doing in my life, in India, and about the work with the street kids. It was an exciting opportunity.

I waved good-bye to my two little girls. I knew they would be okay with my brother and his wife. I would be gone for about twenty-one days. My girls would be busy with school and other activities.

As I prepared to board my flight on October 20, 1995, I was excited. Stuttgart was my first destination. Then I was going to other cities and possibly to Paris.

Now the little girl who dreamed of traveling was actually doing it. My wings of imagination had been replaced with wings of aluminum and steel. I was embarking on an exciting journey. Little did I know how exciting.

The flight was delayed by two and a half hours due to technical difficulties. I became so nervous I almost wanted to run away and not board that flight. I did not know how to back out of that. So I just read and waited for the technical difficulty to be fixed. A little less than two and a half hours passed before we boarded the plane.

I had a lingering, nagging, feeling that all was not going to be well. Oh well, it could be just me.

Before boarding I called my friends Cozi and Heather; a couple that loved me and prayed for me. I told them I sensed all was not well and needed their prayers.

They assured me they would be on their knees till I arrived in Germany and that was an eight hour flight. Friends like them are precious.

The flight was packed. I found my seat and sat down as quickly as I could as I did not want to be in the way. I would make myself comfortable later.

The take-off was uneventful. About an hour into the flight, as we cruised at thirty thousand feet, I opened the screen on the window to see the view. Truthfully, I expected to see nothing but perhaps the stars and the moon, as it was about two in the morning.

Yet I thought there might be the slightest chance of seeing something amazing at that altitude and I did.

It was a huge orange flame.

For a moment, I thought it might be the sun but it was too early in the morning for that. I looked again and realized that the engine was on fire.

We were miles from land, flying over the Indian Ocean. I realized that if we crash landed out here, our chances of survival were slim. My only hope for a safe landing was a miracle.

I heard the dreaded announcement. "We are going to be making an emergency landing. Please remain calm. This is an emergency. We have no time to dump the fuel and will be landing back to the airport with full fuel tanks. Stay calm and fasten your seat belts...." I don't remember all the exact instructions...but in short it meant, "This thing is going to land safely but then it will blow up, so shut up, sit down and stay calm"

My first thoughts raced to my girls. They needed me. All little girls need their mommies. Who would raise them? Only I knew them and loved them more than anyone else in this whole world.

A prayer escaped my lips, "Lord, help me."

Then I thought of the six boys that had adopted me and called me "Mom." Then my mind raced towards all those children at the railway station that waited for me everyday to hug me and be hugged – children who hoped to read and write and have a better future.

The author Jewels Mesaros with the street children in India.

I felt God impressing on my heart to quickly open my Bible and read Psalm 18.

I began to read it loudly, oblivious to the reactions of the fellow passengers. I did not know the contents of that Psalm but obediently read it.

"Praise be to the LORD, I have been delivered from my enemies.

The breakers of death surged round about me; the menacing floods terrified me.

Then the bed of the sea appeared; the world's foundations lay bare, at the roar of the Lord at the storming breath of His nostrils.

He reached down from on high and seized me; drew me out of the deep waters.

He rescued me from my mighty enemy, from foes too powerful for me.

They attacked me on a day of distress, but the LORD came to my support.

He brought me into a spacious place, He set me free in the open; he rescued me because He loves me."

I closed my eyes in thanksgiving knowing that He would come to rescue me. All fear and doubt left as my voice trailed off. Tears of gratitude began to flow to a God who loved me so much.

After the longest twenty minutes of my life, we landed. As we deplaned and boarded the coach I felt an urge to look back at the plane that almost did not make it.

To my surprise the whole plane was tilted to one side. The tires were completely crushed and deflated, the effect of landing on full fuel. And all around there were numerous fire engines – too many to count. I realized they were there just in case the plane blew up.

I smiled. God had kept His Word. He rescued me from an impossible situation. He had a mandate for my life and I made a promise that day that whatever shape His mandate would take in the future I would follow Him wholeheartedly.

The next day I did fly on Lufthansa airways to Germany and had a wonderful twenty one days. He fulfilled His mandate for that season of my life against all odds.

## Notes

_____

_____

_____

_____

_____

_____

_____

_____

_____

_____

_____

_____

_____

_____

_____

_____

_____

_____

_____

_____

_____

_____

_____

# Chapter - 2

## The Miracle of a Doorless Home

The sun shone through my bedroom window facing the east. New frustrations, new tears, new beginnings, new hopes and new challenges pretty much summed up a day in my work with street kids.

Gingerly I got ready to greet the day. Not that I wasn't excited. So much happened in a day with thirty plus children and just two of us volunteering; that a slow morning kind of built up the much needed energy for the day. Fuel for the fire one should think!

As I stepped from the bridge on to the railway platform I was greeted by a bunch of assorted children. They came in all sizes, shapes and ages. Their smiles and gay abandon set my spirit soaring. I knew it was going to be another good day, tears and all!

As we began our day with the literacy program little Lucy tugged at my sleeve, "look", she said, "that lady has been there awhile." I looked up, and just behind the tree in the railway yard sat a lady, emaciated and sad.

I took a break from the class. I went over and sat next to her under the giant mango tree to find out her plight. Her name was Rosie but she had no color in her cheeks, not even a fragrance worth! Haltingly she narrated how she had worked as domestic help for a family for some years.

Now that she was sick they did not want to take care of her and had thrown her out. There were no laws or unions to protect such maids. Rosie whispered weakly, "Can you find me some medical care and help me get back home?" New tears, new fears, new challenges!

My friend Charmaine stood next to me quietly taking everything in. She nodded. That meant that we were in agreement to get her some help. Private nursing homes were much too expensive for a couple of mad caps for God, operating a faith-based ministry.

So we did what was best under the circumstances. We put Rosie in a rickshaw (she could barely walk) and checked her in at the nearest government hospital. Their care wasn't the best but we had to depend on them. Two hours later, after preliminary tests, it was decided by the doctors that Rosie needed fresh blood and at least a couple of days in the hospital.

We left Rosie in the capable hands of medical professionals and headed for home, happy that she would be taken care of and now had a chance to survive. We visited her regularly for a couple of days, but then decided to take a break for a day. The hospital was an hour away from where I lived and with two little children of my own, I was exhausted.

That afternoon I lay in bed enjoying the quiet and listening to the birds in the tall gulmohour tree next to my window. Suddenly I felt impressed in the spirit to go and see Rosie. I began to argue with God. "Not now Lord, I am so tired!" The spiritual nudging grew stronger until I could stand it no more. I telephoned Charmaine and in a couple of minutes we were on our way to the hospital. New challenges, new hopes!

As we got to where Rosie was supposed to be, her bed was taken up by another lady. Rosie was standing in the corner crying and afraid. "Rosie!" I exclaimed, "What's the matter?"

Before she could answer a nurse came up and rudely interjected that Rosie's time was up in the hospital. Someone with a more serious medical condition needed her bed. A mega city has its own share of problems, this was one of them! We had arrived just in time!

Now we had a sick Rosie and no hospital. She had now developed a cyst on her thigh and needed further treatment for that. We did the rounds of a few public hospitals but all were full.

Frustrated, we drove homewards still trying to decide what to do with our sweet Rosie, who by now had become very dear to us. My home had it share of marital problems and bringing her in would not be the best thing. Charmaine lived with her parents and she could not even consider the possibility of asking them.

We called up a couple of our acquaintances who owned spacious houses and asked if they could help. They all said, "No."

It was way past nine and still there was no solution in sight. We bowed our heads in prayer. We looked up and thought about Effie. She had a little hut on the roadside and we didn't have to bother about knocking on her door; she had no door! We stood respectfully outside her tiny house and Charmaine called her gently through the curtain that shielded her and her little family, from the rest of the world.

The curtain parted and there stood Effie wearing a faded blue dress and a bright smile. "What's the matter, sisters?" she said, bewildered to see us out so late.

Effie was about thirty-five years old. Her hair oiled and neatly pulled into a bun. I noticed that her fingers had a lot of cuts. Her hands appeared rough, but as she clasped our hands in hers the warmth of her love and her soft gentle touch melted our apprehensions and fears.

We quickly told her the story. Effie did not hesitate. She motioned us into her humble but warm home. In a few minutes she made up a bed, hugged Rosie and tucked her in.

We heaved a sigh of relief as we waved them both good-bye promising to come and see Rosie the next day. Effie's three little children waved us good-bye. Effie was a single parent.

We soon arrived back at my house. Waving a good bye to Charmaine as she got into a rickshaw, I started to walk back home. The cool breeze blew a wisp of hair on my face. As I brushed it aside, I caught a tear.

Effie lived in a 20 ft x 20 ft hut. She had no house room but she had plenty of heart room and that is what made the difference between a door without miracles and a miracle without doors.

Oh, that we would have no doors on our hearts; we would experience miracles everyday!

## Notes

_____
_____
_____
_____
_____
_____
_____
_____
_____
_____
_____
_____
_____
_____
_____
_____
_____
_____
_____
_____
_____
_____
_____
_____

# Chapter - 3

## The Miracle of A Great Conductor

Charmaine paced around the room. According to her, this was going to be her last day on the face of this earth. The relationship with her mother was almost non-existent. She was the youngest of seven children and no one, not even her dad, had any time for her.

She was forgotten in the midst of every one's busy lifestyle. "No one will miss me," she thought to herself. Deftly, she swung her little niece onto her hip and stepped outside for a last stroll in the backyard.

Her plan was simple. After the stroll, she would hand Jill back to her mother and jump from the top of their apartment building. It would all be over - the pain, the loneliness, this meaningless life.

Charmaine was seventeen years old. She had just completed high school. She was lonely. Her quiet and shy nature had not made her popular. She had few friends. Now to top all that, she was worried about the lump in her breast.

Her mother was too distant emotionally to share her plight. Her sisters were too busy and the age difference between them was so much she felt distanced and alienated from them. There was no way she could ever share this fear with her father and brothers, of course.

A few blocks away, I was busy preparing for a bible study I was going to share with Charmaine. I tidied up my small home, fed my little girls and dressed them to play outside.

Soon it was five o'clock. "Charmaine will be here anytime now," I thought idly to myself. I waited for the doorbell to ring. An hour later, I glanced at the clock. She was late again. There was no sign of her. "Well," I thought, "too many times in the past two months had I waited for her and she did not show up." I really liked Charmaine. We had become close friends and I looked forward to seeing her. I wondered if she just wasn't ready to deal with spiritual issues right now.

I decided to visit her and ask her if she was really interested in her walk with Christ. If she wasn't, we could continue being friends – we would simply discontinue the Bible study part for now.

I asked my neighbor to take care of my girls. I walked to Charmaine's house and knocked at the door. Her father opened the door and beckoned me inside.

At that moment, unbeknownst to me, Charmaine had already placed her niece in the crib and was walking upstairs to the roof top to end her life.

I raced up the stairs excited to see my friend. I hugged her and started narrating some funny incident, not in the least knowing what was going on in her heart. We talked for a while and then I invited Charmaine to come over to my house to enjoy the caramel custard that I had made especially for her.

As we sat in my cozy living room she began to tell me all that she was going through, except the part that she had made a decision to end her life and how it all changed by my sudden visit.

That evening we visited the doctor about the lump in her breast. His prognosis was "nothing serious." I latched on to Charmaine's arm and both walked homewards for some more custard and a fun time with the kids.

Three weeks later Charmaine and I were in a church together. When the minister asked if anyone had a praise report she got up and walked to the platform.

This is the gist of her speech:

"My dear friends in Christ, I thank the Lord for the gift of life. I thank Him, for according to Psalm 139:

The LORD has searched me and He knows me.

He knows when I sit and when I rise; He perceives my thoughts from afar.

He discerns my going out and my lying down; He is familiar with all my ways.

Before a word is on my tongue He knows it completely,

He hems me in - behind and before; He has laid His hand upon me.

Such knowledge is too wonderful for me, too lofty for me to attain.

Where can I go from His Spirit? Where can I flee from His presence?

If I go up to the heavens, He is there; if I make my bed in the depths, He is there.

If I rise on the wings of the dawn, if I settle on the far side of the sea, even there His hand will guide me, His right hand will hold me fast."

She stumbled quickly through the words and with uncertain nervousness, she surveyed the congregation of over two hundred people that sat quietly watching her; then words of gratitude flowed out of her to a God who orchestrates every little detail in our lives.

She told of a friend, a bible study, caramel custard, and perfect timing. God is not subject to time. He created time! Only then did I know the impact that, not mine but God's, perfect timing played in saving her life.

Charmaine went on to graduate from a nursing college and in the last eighteen years has helped heal hundreds of homeless children with wounds in their bodies and hearts.

## Notes

_____

_____

_____

_____

_____

_____

_____

_____

_____

_____

_____

_____

_____

_____

_____

_____

_____

_____

_____

_____

_____

_____

_____

_____

# Chapter - 4
## The Miracle of "Little"

Hand in hand we walked quietly under the shady trees. The six little boys surrounding me seemed like a hedge of hope in this time of deep distress.

Our silence belied the thousands of emotions that stormed inside each one of us. "Little," as we called him, was now pain free. He was just twelve years old and had gone ahead of each one of us to a better place.

I remembered the first time I saw him – a tattered sheet wrapped around him. It was New Year's Eve. I was out on my usual jaunt to see if any child needed help. There he was. He seemed to be in pain.

Street children his age would normally be begging or playing. He sat quietly, his eyes filled with pain. Tears trickled down his tender cheeks. We talked quietly together.

All he knew was that his name was "Little". He haltingly narrated his story. When he was about four years old someone kidnapped and left him in a city of almost twelve million people. He couldn't remember anything about his family or where he came from.

As he narrated his story, he lifted his sheet and showed me a gaping wound on the left upper thigh. I decided to take him to the hospital. After various tests it was determined that he had sickle cell anemia and bone tuberculosis. "Phew!" I thought to myself. Not wanting to put him in a public hospital, I defied all financial odds and had him admitted to a private hospital.

Two months later, "Little" had not only recovered substantially, he had won the hearts of every doctor and nurse on his floor. It was time now to go home.

Till now he always called me "sister." As we waited for a cab, he spotted one and suddenly said, "Mom, there is a cab!" No further gestures or words were necessary. An adoption took place, without any papers, right there in the middle of a busy street! Little had adopted me.

Little's life made it possible for these children to come live with us.

Other "sons" of mine still lived out on the streets and needed a home. Maybe it was time. God's perfect time! Like checks being cashed in a bank, all the prayers made in the last five years suddenly broke through. In less than forty-eight hours we received enough money to pay Little's hospital bills.

Additionally God provided for a deposit and eleven months rent in advance for a Boy's Home. Someone had recently got married and even decided to give us some furniture to from their wedding presents!

As we arranged the furniture, the sun shone brightly on Little. "Mom," he said, "I would like you to stop calling me 'Little'". He caught me by surprise. "Ok Little, for the last time I call you 'Little." What would you like to be called, Little"? I teased. He grinned and the dimples on his cheek deepened. I tousled his hair and gave him a hug. He really was hardly little anymore. He had put on about 15 pounds and wore a belt to support his back that made him look like a Police Officer.

All the other boys gathered around us and we sat taking a welcome break from all the shifting and pushing. "Mom," said one of the boys, "how about 'Prem'?" *Prem* means *Love* and another quipped "*Sagar,*" meaning *Ocean.* 'Sagar' was perfect too. We decided to use both. Prem Sagar became Little's new name.

God's ocean of love had made it possible for us to have a Boy's Home and the rent, the furniture and everything else we needed. Besides Little's heart was always so full of love for all his "brothers" and me that any other name would be unfitting.

"Prem Sagar," the sign-board outside the little orphanage stood as a mute testimony of a boy who showed how to love, be loved, and keep smiling against all odds. While the doctors healed bodies, Prem Sagar healed hearts during his short three month stay at that hospital.

A severe bout of chicken pox combined with sickle cell anemia did not give him much chance despite the best medical facilities. His earthly life was cut short but Prem Sagar made it possible for a dream to take wings.

It was time for Prem to wish us good-bye. He wanted to be a Police Officer he once told me, to help street kids. Well, he was more than a police officer; he was God's angel in the right place at the right time!

Prem Sagar was the beginning of a home for many street kids. Many found refuge there from the grueling heat and cruelty of a mega city that was wrapped in its own poverty and dire needs.

Prem Sagar made it possible to bring a piece of heaven on earth, to desperate children in need.

## Notes

_____

_____

_____

_____

_____

_____

_____

_____

_____

_____

_____

_____

_____

_____

_____

_____

_____

_____

_____

_____

_____

_____

_____

_____

# Chapter - 5

## The Miracle of Perfect Timing

For the third time that evening I tried to make the computer work. The honeysuckle was in full bloom and its fragrance evoked a verse for a new poem as it wafted in through the open window. I was eager to write.

Exasperated, I decided to visit the engineer who worked at the small hardware store on the corner of my block. I hesitated a moment as I looked at the time. My teenage daughter had gone to visit with our next door neighbor. I was wondering if I should wait for her to come back.

Then I recalled the brief conversation on the phone with the engineer, "… bring the machine around eight or so tonight or tomorrow morning." I glanced at my wrist watch. It was only six-thirty.

Somehow, something, far greater than the present situation urged me to step out.

I walked out of my gate onto the busy street. A few years ago it was a lonely road. Now a movie theater, few restaurants, a Dominos Pizza place and so many other facilities had taken over the quiet neighborhood. Quiet would not describe it now.

As I quickened my pace to avoid the noise and pollution, a woman waved at me. In an instant I knew. It was a divine appointment. It was time for a miracle.

I quickly took in the woman's appearance. She was hungry and thirsty. Carrying a heavy bag and a little baby was taking its toll on the woman. The child was about two years old, malnourished and listless.

I gently placed my hand on the woman's shoulder, "What is the matter"? I asked.

"I came from a village to look for my husband," she replied in frustration. "He is a construction worker. I had this address but he is not there anymore. They have shifted him to another site. I don't know his new address. We don't have a place to live." She then pointed to her sister across the road, an older lady. She had another little girl with her about five years old.

I beckoned her to come over. Apprehension writ large on her face, the woman gingerly walked towards us. The younger one quickly filled her in with the details of our meeting.

I silently lifted my heart to God and asked Him what He wanted me to do. "Ask them if you could pray with them," I heard Him say. I was quite sure that they would be skeptical. Judging from their appearance the name of Christ would be foreign to them, but I thought to myself that I would follow my impression and pray with them.

As I told them what I was going to do their faces lit up. "Oh," the older woman said, "we know Him. We have a prayer meeting at our house once a week." Tears streamed down her eyes as she looked heavenward and began to give thanks to a God who cared.

The cars zipped by as we sat under a tree in the twilight hour. The mosquitoes were relentlessly trying to devour us. In spite of the situation, we expressed our faith in God and praised Him for His faithfulness to us.

After we said, "amen," I asked them how I could help. They talked for a moment together and then said that it would be great if I could get them tickets to go back to their town.

We hailed a cab and got to the railway station. I purchased their tickets and put a few rupees in their hands for food on their journey. Both the women hugged me, one on either side. For a moment I felt the arms of God around me and remembered the scripture, "Inasmuch as you have done unto the least of these…"

In a few minutes the train came chugging around the bend. We bid fervent goodbyes. I turned around and walked into the night smiling to myself.

Two women and their little babies would be safe tonight. My thoughts trailed to whether she would find her husband. I smiled again knowing that He was the God of perfect timing. He would do it in His time.

# Notes

_____

_____

_____

_____

_____

_____

_____

_____

_____

_____

_____

_____

_____

_____

_____

_____

_____

_____

_____

_____

_____

# Chapter - 6

## The Miracle of Kisses

It was a cold wintry morning. And like an old poem I knew as a child, it came back afresh. "The North wind does blow and we shall have snow."

This winter was exceptionally cold. I was still getting used to the cold climate. It was a big change from my equatorial surroundings in India. I looked out of the local bus and his walk caught my eye.

He was about twenty-two years old, lean, and had a limp. Not dressed warmly enough for the chill weather. He stretched out his hand to the next person passing him by. All he got was a "no".

I quickly alighted at the next stop and walked back towards my destination that morning. I intended to meet him. He had by then reached a traffic light and both of us were inadvertently stopped by the red signal. When the light turned green, I waited for him to come towards me.

He could barely move his right hand and right leg. He walked slowly and dragged his steps. As he neared me I smiled. He smiled back. "Hey", I said "Good morning. My name is Jewels."

His eyes lit up and he said, "The name is Dennis, Ma'am." I slowed my pace to walk with him. I asked him if he would like some breakfast. "Sure," he said. "Will you buy me some breakfast from the little café down the street? I love that place…they give you refill coffee."

I knew which café he was talking about. It was going to be a long walk. As we walked, he told me his story. He was homeless. He had lost his father when he was five. He lost the use of his arm and leg in a car accident when he was nine.

The next thing he said was, "Give me a kiss, just one kiss!" We walked further I ignored him. My kisses were reserved for the love of my life. As we continued to walk he just kept punctuating everything he said with, "Give me a kiss, just one kiss!"

Without even entertaining his persistent request in my thoughts, I kept walking with him to the little café. Making light hearted conversation I kept reminding him that my kisses were reserved for someone special.

Finally we reached the café and I bought him some breakfast. As I helped him with the tray he said, "Give me a kiss, just one kiss!"

I smiled. Keeping the tray on the table, I sat opposite him. For a moment he concentrated on his breakfast. "It's good Ma'am, I ain't had nothin' since lunch yesterday and man, this coffee will keep me warm."

When he was done with his breakfast I excused myself and got up to greet the remaining part of the day. "Bye, Dennis. Have a good day and take care," I said. He waved and as I walked outside I heard his voice drifting. And his last words were, "Give me a kiss, just one kiss!"

I did a number of different things that day. I took a ferry ride, walked on an island, did some window shopping and just enjoyed the day.

His words though, kept ringing in my ears, "Give me a kiss." He did not ask for any money. He did not ask for a pair of pants or a sweater. He did not even ask for an expensive breakfast. When I asked him what kind of breakfast he would like to have, he chose the cheapest.

I wondered what the kiss was all about. Then as if a movie was switched on in my head I began to see all the times I was kissed and all the times I kissed.

I had two lovely daughters and we never left the house without kissing each other. Bed time came to my mind and I thought how we always said goodnight with three kisses. One for every cheek and a sweet little lip kiss.

I remembered the time I had to go on a twenty day trip. My girls sat me down and both kissed me sixty times each and then I did the same for them. So we were going to be good and all filled with kisses for the next twenty days.

He didn't know he was being improper; it was just about being loved. It was just that simple.

I realized that he was looking for something that was missing in his life. Perhaps the one kiss his daddy never gave him before he died.

Perhaps it was the one kiss his mother couldn't give him before she gave him up for adoption.

Perhaps it was the one kiss that eluded him and left him empty and longing for the greatest gift of all, love.

I thought about Dennis as I lay myself in bed that night and prayed that an angel might visit him to give him his mother's last kiss - a gentle touch from God.

## Notes

_____

_____

_____

_____

_____

_____

_____

_____

_____

_____

_____

_____

_____

_____

_____

_____

_____

_____

_____

_____

_____

_____

_____

# Chapter - 7

## The Miracle of a Quick Prayer

Ah! Saturday! I could sleep in. Gingerly, I opened one eye to look at my little kitty scrambling over my nice clean sheets.

I reached over for the newspaper that was left for me. Things hadn't been right in our city for a few weeks now, and I eagerly wanted to know what was going on.

What I read sent chills down my spine.

"Eighteen people killed in violence - city of Bombay. Police said the violence began late on Friday night and escalated into a mob fight... police finally dispersed the crowds and imposed a curfew at the scene of the fighting, which also left fifteen people dead, fifteen wounded including eleven policemen... Officials said the atmosphere was still tense but under control."

My heart raced towards the street kids that I knew. I wondered how they were doing. Were they safe? How were they coping? I wanted to run to meet them but, because of the curfew, I had to wait. Obviously, none of them had cell phones, or any other contact number. I just had to wait and pray.

As the mood eased in the city that weekend, things got better. The curfew was lifted and I could visit the children on Tuesday.

As soon as I got to the railway station I was greeted by a bunch of teenagers that I worked with. I knew they would have plenty of stories to tell me. They always loved to hang on to my arm and tell me all that was going on. Today, I thought they would probably have some more exciting stuff, but nothing prepared me for what I was going to hear.

Bobby, our oldest, silenced everyone and had us sit on the steps of the railway yard guards' room. The railway police were kind and let us use the steps as a classroom as long as we cleaned up after ourselves. Bobby was the oldest and he took charge of the conversation. He had something important to share.

Unseen Heroes

He began quietly, "Last night as I was walking near the railway tracks (that's where all the children lived) I saw a few men in the dark, laying thick cables across the railway track. All of a sudden I realized that that their intent was to derail the train. A similar incident occurred a few days ago at another station. Over thirty-five had died and many injured. I quickly looked at the railway clock and knew there would be another packed train coming in less than five minutes.

The train would be filled with people returning home from work", he said. "I broke into a sweat knowing that it would be the last day for many people if I did not act." Eyes wide, he continued, "The minutes ticked by. I realized that if I ran to the railway office no one would believe me, a street kid. But if I waited longer, it would be a real disaster.

Suddenly I saw a couple of my friends and yelled to hurry up and we started running towards each other. One of them said to me, "What's the matter? Looks like you have seen a ghost!" I quickly told them what I had seen and then like a wave it hit me – we can pray. The four of us closed our eyes and said a quick prayer. "Lord Jesus, save the innocent – perform a miracle!" I was going to ramble on when I heard the sound of the train approaching and we all moved to a safer spot.

It was an express train; which meant that it would not make a stop at this station. It would be hurtling along at great speed to the next station. As it zipped by, we just closed our eyes and continued to pray. A few seconds later we heard it rumble by and it went on its way uninterrupted".

Bobby had now finished his story and the boys and girls started clapping and cheering for him. I hugged him real tight and said he was a hero! He just smiled and pointed heavenwards and said, "God did it".

As the afternoon sun melted into long evening shadows, I walked back home. I realized that Bobby had taken a risk to pray instantly in front of his friends to save strangers. Bobby was as much a hero as if he had jumped in front of the train to stop it.

I also knew that if I called up a newspaper and told them this story they wouldn't think it worth printing. "No hard evidence," they would say. This wasn't sensational stuff in the eyes of the world. It wasn't an act of great bravery using Herculean strength or the courage of a lion. It would be ridiculed – or just ignored.

It was almost dark by the time I reached the gate to my house. I stopped to take in the quiet of the evening and waited to hear a cricket or two. It was a busy day and much had happened. I heard a little bird chirp and looked up into the tree and from the corner of my eye I saw a shooting star.

As my gaze lifted further upwards it dawned on me that in the great portals of heaven was a book where the faithful acts of even little children were recorded and one day my hero, Bobby would hear the applause of heaven.

I walked in closed my door on a busy troubled world and opened my heart in thanksgiving to a God who hears and answers the prayers of our spiritual heroes.

Well done, Bobby!

*Notes*

_____

_____

_____

_____

_____

_____

_____

_____

_____

_____

_____

_____

_____

_____

_____

_____

_____

_____

_____

_____

_____

_____

_____

_____

# Chapter - 8

## The Miracle of the Dining Table

I picked the last box that was to go out of the door. In less than an hour we would be in our new home. The curtains that were still on the rod seem to wave a last goodbye as the westerly sea winds kissed them gently.

Looking around for the last time I was overcome with mixed emotions. I was happy to be moving into a bigger place but I was sad to leave so many memories behind.

I sat on a chair that was going to be left behind for the next owner. I motioned for my children to leave and that I would join them in a few minutes. They left with their aunt to get into the van.

The only other piece of furniture was a dining table. I smiled as I began to relive the stories around that table. This table had to go because it did not fit into the décor of the new home. I had thought of giving it to my two young nieces who would continue the legacy of the dining table that traveled around the world – almost!

Ten years ago I had a group of teenage missionaries come to the city of Bombay. They were a vivacious bunch filled with excitement for the unknown and so eager to explore this city with twelve million people.

This city of Bombay in India was a potpourri of people from different states. Diverse and interesting, like a thousand different flowers simmering in a hundred different oils.

Their one month stay ended too quickly and on their last day they gave us this large dining table as a parting gift that could seat eight people.

In a few weeks I had visitors from Alaska. Somewhere in the middle of the year I had visitors from France and Switzerland; then a family from Korea with their twins; then a wonderful young couple all the way from Sweden.

Then, five years ago, a group of eighteen young adults from Australia had tea with us (when they say *tea* they mean *dinner)*. I invited them for tea and they wouldn't leave even at six o'clock. Finally I asked them where they would be having dinner and they looked at me quizzically. The leader of the group explained that tea time in Australia meant dinner.

Everyone started to laugh and then I quickly got to work to fix dinner for eighteen hungry young adults. We all squeezed around the miracle table and ate that simple but hot dinner. As they waved their goodbyes that night each gave me a tight hug and whispered, "thank you".

I remembered all the times my boys came home to eat. Each one was so special. We had all adopted each other. At that table, all differences seem to melt away. Somehow history was eradicated for a few moments.

I had found Vishal eating out of garbage outside a restaurant five years ago. Shanky, I had found wandering at a railway station.

Their faces and so many others just kept coming to my mind. Over ten years of apprehension, joy, praise, and thankfulness all sort of rolled up in two words, sharing and caring!

It was a table of the impossibles made possible. We discussed how God was faithful. How we could trust Him through the difficulties. How He kept us from sickness and disease when we were on an assignment from Him. How He could heal, should we need His gentle touch. Along with the aroma of food, prayers rose to heaven from that table – and were answered.

The table seemed to echo the giggles of little children and the laughter of teenagers and young adults. It resonated with gentle drops of tears that come with goodbyes. I knew some of them I would never see again. A table full of memories that moving away from it could not erase the imprints it had left behind. I felt that the joy that it would bring to my nieces was untold.

Someone banged at the door and I awoke from this day dreaming. I smiled as I got up. I could have cried, but I decided to smile, as I thought about the stories I would tell my nieces and pass on the tradition of hospitality and extreme joy.

Indeed it was a table that traveled around the world including heaven.

My miracle dining table!

## Notes

_____

_____

_____

_____

_____

_____

_____

_____

_____

_____

_____

_____

_____

_____

_____

_____

_____

_____

_____

_____

_____

_____

_____

_____

# Chapter - 9
## The Miracle of the Embrace

The hot sun peeked through the thick canopy of leaves. The little mango blossoms were almost ready to burst forth with new fruit.

One of the blossoms fell on the crayons that were lined ready to be picked up by a group of children who would drop in at our little open air mobile school. I whisked it away with my finger tip and got ready for my young charges.

Three times a week we laid out mats on the dirt and held school in the railway yard. Children came willingly for a couple of hours to color and to learn to read and write. Many of them – even as old as twelve years old – had never ever held a crayon much less filled a coloring book. For some of them it was an exciting time to learn, others just liked to sit and hear the stories.

Some days, class was nothing but singing and dancing. Some days we just did clownish things. I had to find ways to bring a smile to the faces of these children that never knew a hot meal or a soft bed or for many of them, the love of a mother or father.

They all had a rough life. No home to start with. Many of them were abandoned or had run away from their home. Some were as young as seven.

The conditions by the railway track and yard were appalling; not a place where anyone should live, let alone children.

The railway station was convenient, though. They could meet friends at other railway stations and share their problems or help one another. They had an amazing network.

They could also board a train and travel without a ticket any time. The railway police found it hard to catch them as they were more agile than the adults. Also the railway platforms had lots of little cafeterias and once in awhile, a kind soul would buy them a meal or they could eat out of the trash.

For these little children *railway* was synonymous with *life*.

Life was hard for them, so our little mobile school was a kind of oasis. Besides some basic reading and writing skills, we also gave them a hearty snack. The children loved it and made it a point not to miss class.

One day, Jay was missing. He was the one with dark curly hair and big brown eyes. He was only five or six years old. Occasionally he would smile shyly and you could see a set of perfectly white teeth. He loved to color and most days he would just take his little coloring book and color away. He never spoke a word.

All I knew about his family history was that his parents were really old. He had a little sister about a year old. His dad was an alcoholic. I often saw him lying sprawled on the railway platform. His mother looked about sixty. It could have been just her hard life and the constant abuse. She always waved at me whenever she saw me. I hadn't seen her either for a couple of days.

I enquired about Jay from the other children. They said they had not seen him. We carried on with our class as usual. With every child that came in, I expected to see Jay. He never showed up.

A day later we were back on the mat, teaching, telling stories, bandaging wounds, and sharing hugs. Jay was still missing.

I was concerned about him. The children had enough of their own stuff to deal with than wonder where Jay was. The fact that he never spoke a word did not help. When class was over I began to pack.

Just then I felt a tap on my back. There he was with his big brown eyes and a tender smile. Like I said before Jay never ever spoke. All he did was stare or smile. So even if I asked him where he was I would not get an answer.

I turned around to pick him up and he winced. He had a huge bruise on his arm. I didn't know whether he fell or someone beat him. Even if I found out, I could do little about it. The system was not set up to handle child abuse.

Gently I picked him up and cradled him. I had seen him many times before. I had waved at him, tried to include him the class but he was always painfully shy. Today he let me pick him up without protest. He lay in the crook of my arm as if he belonged there and shut his eyes. I started to hum a lullaby. I patted his hair and stroked his cheek lovingly. I continued to rock him.

A few minutes later his eyes still closed I saw tiny tears trickling down his little cheeks. I kept humming and kept rocking. The tears flowed from his eyes.

It was more than hour and then the tears dried as sure as they had started. He got up and without a word walked towards his home that was nothing but an open space on the railway platform.

I let him go. I would have loved to hold him longer but seemed that was all he needed for today. We had talked volumes without speaking a single word. That encounter was forever impressed on my heart and mind.

Often times when I am lonely or hurting, I think about Jay and then remember that my Father in heaven holds me in the crook of His arm and keeps me there till I feel all better again.

Thank you Jay for letting me embrace you. You gave me much more than I could ever give you.

## Notes

_____

_____

_____

_____

_____

_____

_____

_____

_____

_____

_____

_____

_____

_____

_____

_____

_____

_____

_____

_____

_____

_____

_____

_____

# Chapter - 10

## The Miracle of the Helpers

The crowd was thick around me. It was peak traveling time and the people jostled all about. Nearly five million people travel everyday by the local trains in Bombay. Walking down the railway platform it seemed that there were nearly a million people around me.

I was trying to take two steps at a time to get to the other side of the bridge where the street kids were waiting for me. It would be less busy and somewhat out of way of all the pushing and shoving. My days were filled with the hugs and love of these children who had nothing – and yet everything to give. Here, in these desperate circumstances, a little love went a long way.

As I reached the top of the bridge, I was horrified to see an old man curled in a fetal position. The stench that arose from his surroundings was unbearable.

He was steeped in his own excrement and people were just holding their noses and walking past him. He was probably lying there overnight or longer.

I was appalled. I had not, in my many years in this city, seen anything like that.

One look at him and I did an about turn to go take the other bridge so I could avoid the smell. As I made my escape, I heard the Lord whisper, "Jewels, your turning away will not change his circumstances. Go back. Go back and help him."

I hesitated. How on earth was I going to help him? I wasn't a big strong man; I did not have a gurney and there was no 911 number I could call for help. So many excuses – and they were darn good ones – but I knew better than to argue with God.

I walked back slowly not taking two steps at a time now. I was pondering how I was going to remedy this impossible situation. The only thing I knew was that I had to go back. How it would all play out was to be seen.

I stooped over holding my breath to see if he was alive. All of a sudden a man appeared and said, "Sister can I help you?" He was one of the regular homeless at the railway station.

"Yes, I need your help." I was really glad that he asked. So as we were talking trying to find a solution two other men stopped and said that they would also to help this unfortunate man.

Now all of a sudden there were three helpers! We could not transfer him to a local hospital in this condition. He needed a clean up and some new clothes.

I quickly opened my purse and handed some money to get towels and a pair of pants and shirt. I had never seen the man in my life and in a few minutes he had disappeared with the entire amount. I wasn't worried; this was a divine appointment.

While he was gone on his errand, the other two carried the man out of the way of the passers by. The helper did return with the clothes, just as I had expected. They borrowed a bucket of water from a stall and cleaned the man and dressed him up. In about half an hour he was ready to be transported to a local hospital.

In all that time all I did was watch a miracle unfold. A miracle of the hearts of strangers knit together by a God of compassion working through His gentle willing helpers.

I knew the one who first asked to help; the other two I had never seen before and have never seen again. Even more importantly the ones that He was working through were almost as unfortunate as the victim.

"Better" people apparently had "better" things to do. Except for the mercy and grace of God, I was almost one of them.

*Notes*

_____

_____

_____

_____

_____

_____

_____

_____

_____

_____

_____

_____

_____

_____

_____

_____

_____

_____

_____

_____

_____

_____

_____

# Chapter - 11

## *The Miracle of Hope*

The flight was ready for take off. Everyone was in their seats and just as the crew was getting ready to close the door of the aircraft in walked a petite figure – no more than five feet tall and very frail. I assumed she weighed about hundred and ten pounds or thereabouts. She had more the appearance of a child than a grown woman.

Something didn't seem right about her. She sat across the aisle from me and immediately lowered her head. Tears were streaming down her face.

After take off, I asked the man next to her if he would exchange seats with me. He obliged. I sat next to her and gently tapped her on the shoulder. Tears were still streaming down her face. They seem to come from a bottomless well in her little heart.

We got talking and in between her sobs and muffles she told me her life story. As her life began to unfold, I had to pinch myself to see that I was not watching a horror movie made by a completely twisted mind.

Sara was born in a tiny village in northern India. She was the only child of aged parents. Though old and conservative in many ways, they understood the need of some education for the apple of their eye.

The nearest school was about a mile and half away. Sara walked both ways as in this remote village there were no school buses and hardly any other means of transportation.

One bright summer, she remembered running home all the way from school because her mother was going to make her favorite dessert. As she neared the door she heard some voices. Puzzled, she peeped in to see a young man probably in his late twenties talking to her dad. Thinking it might have been someone new in the village she hurried to the back door. Her mother called her in and introduced her to the young man.

Sara's heart began to beat fast. Were they trying to match-make? She was only fifteen. That would not be unusual as some of her friends were already engaged. But Sara had dreams. She dreamed of finishing school going to college and then someday being a teacher.

Her dad's loud voice soon jolted her back to reality. The boy, Babu, seemed pleasant but she was not ready yet.

The next day as she was going to school, he followed her. Soon they were talking and before long, he completely won her over. He told her stories about the city. He told her how she could continue to study once she was his wife and let her old parents take a break from the financial burden of educating her. Sara consented and she was married that year. Her nightmare had just begun.

Babu took her to the city. He did not have a house. They constantly lived in a shabby motel. Almost every evening he would lock her in the motel and go off to drink and would not return until the wee hours of the morning.

He occasionally took her shopping. She was never allowed to go anywhere by herself. She often wrote to her parents. Not wanting them to worry, she wrote she was happy. Besides, Babu always read her letters. There was no way of escape.

Five months later, Babu went on a trip to the Middle East. He gave her just enough money for survival and told her he would be back in two weeks. She was terrified to be left alone but at least there was now a glimmer of hope for escape.

Once Babu left, she realized she was pregnant and with the little money she had, she left for her hometown. It was a long journey but worth it. Eight and a half months later she gave birth to a little boy. Months passed with no word from Babu. She was glad that Babu was not coming back, or so it seemed.

A year later he came to take her back. Tradition and culture demanded that she go with him. Babu insisted that they leave their son behind as the environment was better in the village. Sara's parents happily obliged. Sara left with Babu, following like a sheep to the slaughter.

Sara hated her life. She longed for her little boy. She often spent time crying while Babu was away drinking. Then one day he told her he had to go back to the Middle East and he would be back in a couple of weeks.

After he left Sara befriended an older lady who lived across from the motel. She advised her to get financially independent and take up a job as a maid in the Middle East. Sara went job hunting and found an agency that would help her out.

She sold her gold ornaments for a passport, visa and ticket. A week later she was on her first flight. It almost seemed like she had wings and was flying to her freedom forever. Babu would never find her.

On her arrival at the airport she was happy that her employer had sent her a car to pick her up. In a few minutes she arrived at this huge house that looked to her like a palace. Once inside, she was shoved into one small room with three other girls about her age. Tired and worn out from the long journey she went to bed. She would get her answers in the morning.

The next day she was asked to dress up real pretty and was taken in a fancy car to a hotel. She asked her driver when she would have to start work. Stone faced, he replied, "Very soon".

She sat in the hotel room alone and in a few minutes, two men entered the room, raped her and left. Sara was numb. What had she gotten herself into? That evening another man came and raped her. It went on through the night. A few days later she was shifted to another hotel and the nightmare continued. Sometime as many as fifteen to twenty men would rape her in a day. It did not take Sara long to realize she was trapped. Her passport had been taken. Her wings were clipped.

This nightmare continued for about eight months. Almost every few days she was in a new hotel with new girls. A brothel madam would come in and handpick one of them for the next customer.

It was the month of August and about the eight month of her ordeal. A brothel madam came in, looked at her and went out almost immediately. She came back and asked Sara if she was Babu's wife.

Sara could not make sense. How would this lady know? She was in a foreign country and no one knew her whereabouts. She was wrong.

In a few minutes the door opened and in walked Babu. He was livid. He wept and ranted and raved all at the same time. Suddenly through his ranting and raving Sara understood that he was a ring leader of a large flesh trade.

No wonder he was always gone. He never really worked but always had money. This lady was Babu's sister and though Sara had never seen her she had seen Babu's wedding picture.

Everything fell into place. Sara had innocently applied for a job like thousands of other girls and fell into this trap; a trap her husband never dreamed his wife would fall into.

He cursed her and told her she was no longer his wife. He made a phone call to her group leader and got her passport and put her on the plane. As she reached the airport he said, "We are no longer husband and wife. You are just another prostitute. Go home and kill yourself. You are not worthy to live!"

As Sara finished her story, I put my arms around her. She sobbed bitterly. I had no answers to her future. I knew that there weren't any organizations that could help her, and besides, I thought she might want to go home to her son.

As the flight landed, I asked her to stay with me through the luggage check. Gathering our luggage we headed for some tea. She was still crying. Her tears never stopped. I asked her if she wanted to go back to her home town. She told me she did, but did not have any money.

On the first leg of my flight, a gentleman had given me four hundred and fifty rupees – equivalent to about ten dollars – as a donation towards the work with the street kids. I smiled to myself. Sara needed that money and it was provided to me for her. Nevertheless, I knew that it would not be enough.

I remembered the new gold earrings that I just brought on this trip. I took them off and along with the money, handed it over to Sara. These earrings were meaningless to me in the present situation. They were not as important to me as what they could do for her.

Hugging her tightly I asked her if I could pray for her. I did not need an answer; she just closed her eyes. I prayed that evening through my tears asking God to protect her and lead her towards healing and wholeness.

We exchanged addresses. I never ever heard from Sara. I often wonder about her and the millions of girls caught up in the flesh trade.

I got back home and into the normal schedule of things, one of them being to continue to work with children that were destitute and orphaned.

Sara made my determination all the more firm and my calling all the more clear.

God often moves in mysterious ways, but speaks clearly. To me, Sara was His voice to bring hope to the hopeless in the midst of a broken and dying world.

Hope for the girls who almost never get a chance at education.

## Notes

_____

_____

_____

_____

_____

_____

_____

_____

_____

_____

_____

_____

_____

_____

_____

_____

_____

_____

_____

_____

_____

_____

_____

_____

# Chapter - 12

## *The Miracle of Forgiveness*

It was an unexpectedly sunny day. The wild daisies on the plains in front of beckoned to come and smell them. I got off my mountain bike and inhaled the sweet fragrance. For a moment I forgot all my pain and tears.

I smiled taking in the fresh white and brilliant yellow. Somehow it reminded me of my childhood. The huge Indian honeysuckle tree outside my little house was a constant source of joy. I would sit beneath its shade with my books for hours and enjoy the shower of those little flowers softly kissing me as they fell to the ground.

A wild bird called and I was back to reality. A sigh escaped my lips. So much had happened in the past twenty-seven years. I remembered the white roses in my wedding bouquet. Then I remembered the white lilies on my mother's casket soon after. I remembered the day I walked into the court and I remembered the sunflowers smiling at the sun as I faced I thought, a bleak future.

I mounted my bike and began pedaling at top speed. I parked the bike inside my garage and ran to the shower. In less than half hour I would have to be at the bus stop.

The highlight of my week was visiting downtown Seattle. I loved the busy waterfront. The crowded market place always reminded me of my homeland thousands of miles away in the Far East. Best of all I liked the Northwest flowers in all their glory.

The glorious sight of the dried and fresh flowers lined up at the Pike Place Market rejuvenated me. I always smiled a little more and my eyes always seem to sparkle a little more after the colorful encounters.

As I walked toward the market, I thought about my life. I wished things were different. I had made too many mistakes and was in a mess. I was sure God was disappointed in me. Looking heavenward, I wondered if there was really such a thing as total forgiveness.

Hastily I crossed the street to meet my friend Maggie who worked at the little vegetable shop on the corner. On reaching the shop, I looked around to find her, but could not see Maggie anywhere. There was just a lone gentleman minding the little store.

I cleared my throat to draw his attention. He stopped arranging the vegetables. "Yes Ma'am, what can I do for you"? I asked about Maggie. "Maggie has taken a day off."

"Ok, I answered, "please tell her that I was here." extending my hand I introduced myself, "Jewels."

Without blinking, the man held out his hand and said, "Forgiven."

I couldn't believe my ears. "What did you say"?

"Forgiven," he replied. "Forgiven is my name." He turned away and continued with his work, not realizing the impact he had on my heart.

Tears welled up in my eyes and spilled down my cheeks. They flowed faster than I could wipe them. The love of the Father flooded my being. How many times does one meet a man named Forgiven?

I walked out of the market, tears still blurring my vision but in my heart it was spring as I inhaled the sweet and unforgettable scent of Forgiveness.

## *Notes*

_____

_____

_____

_____

_____

_____

_____

_____

_____

_____

_____

_____

_____

_____

_____

_____

_____

_____

_____

_____

_____

_____

_____

_____

_____

# Chapter - 13
## *The Miracle of Mili*

As I stepped out of the house on to the driveway I saw her. There she was with her back arched as if she would tear her enemy into shreds at any minute. She was just a little kitten. Her enemy was a dog almost four feet high. Boy, was she courageous! Picking her up, I put her inside the safety of the gate. I did not want to loose her again.

My mind raced back to yesterday. Only twenty-four hours ago, she was in a near death situation.

It was a bright sunny day as it often was in a tropical city like Bombay in the colorful nation of India. After finishing my appointment with the dentist, I stepped out of the clinic and walked a few meters. There, right in the middle of the road, lying perfectly still, was a white and black form. It was a tiny frail kitten. I bent over her nearly lifeless body and looked around if someone knew how she got there. My heart went out to her.

A burly man came up to me and said, "She is sick." Before I could utter a word of protest, he picked her up by the neck and threw her to the other side of the road.

I glared at him. He did not seem to notice and went about whatever he was doing.

Quickly I ran across to the crumpled furry form. There did seem to be some life left in her. I could see her little rib cage rise and fall very feebly. It seemed that every breath would be her last.

Without further thought, I ran across to a store and bought some water in a small cup. I knelt over her and splashed a few drops on her tiny pink nose. She opened her eyes ever so slowly. Then she made a gentle attempt to get up and drink some water that I held for her. I was overjoyed to see signs of life.

I ran back to the store to buy some milk. They had nothing except some strawberry milk. I didn't think she cared. She was so dehydrated. Anything at this point would help. Then I ran across to another store to buy a small saucer.

I glanced at the spot where she lay. She was sitting up! I quickly emptied the entire contents of the strawberry milk into the saucer. For some strange reason unknown to me, I have always hated the flavor and smell of strawberries but at that time the scent was the scent of love and life.

She lapped it up quickly and then tried to walk around. Having revived her, I decided to stand up. She began to purr ever so feebly. I could hardly hear her!

She tried to rub herself against my leg and weakly sat down again. But she looked up as if to say, "thank you."

I smiled and decided since all was well with her, I could go home now. As I started to walk she feebly tried to follow me.

I turned and there she was. I did not know that I was an orphan, but I must have been because now I was adopted! This little kitten had decided to adopt me as her mom.

I hesitated for a moment, then picked her little frail body in my hand and headed home. I named her "Mili" which, in Hindi, means "found".

She not only recovered quickly, but in less than twenty-four hours she was taking on a dog – her natural enemy hundred times her size! Now, that was a brave little kitten!

As I look back on that incident I realize it does not take much to give – even to restore a life. We often do not stop for a simple act of kindness even for our fellow human beings, because it may take too much from us.

We are afraid it will cost us too much money, time and internal resources, but sometimes just a little bit from us can make a great big difference between life and death to someone else.

Mili did not need much. She just needed a little loving, some strawberry milk and she was ready to take on the world!

## Notes

_____

_____

_____

_____

_____

_____

_____

_____

_____

_____

_____

_____

_____

_____

_____

_____

_____

_____

_____

_____

_____

_____

_____

# Chapter - 14

## *The Miracle of a Card*

It had been raining hard all night. Just like any other bleak wintry day I had no desire to get out of bed but I did not want to be late to church either. My mother's words were ringing in my ears. "You can be late anywhere, but never to church!" Thirty years had passed since I last heard it but, somehow, every Sunday her voice rang afresh in my ears. I scrambled hastily out of bed; took a quick shower, brushed my teeth, dressed and dashed out of the door.

Church was just a few blocks away, so I walked as I usually did. That wintry morning, a cold draft reminded me of my brother whom I had not spoken to in over a year. We were three siblings. All grown up now, we were separated due to choices we had made in our lives. I thought about cold hearts. Hearts that would not yield to unconditional love, hearts which would love only if we met their expectations.

As I increased my pace, I thought of my little niece who I had taught to walk. Now she was fifteen years old and I hadn't spoken to her in over two years. I remembered her dimpled cheeks and button nose. She must be a pretty teenager, I thought.

As I increased my pace, I almost slipped on the frozen sidewalk. Over the years, barriers like huge glaciers had developed between my brother and me. How was I going to thaw them?

It would be a monumental task.

As I reached the entrance of the church, my thoughts melted in the warm atmosphere. During the worship service, I decided to concentrate on a God who was able and willing to make molehills out of mountains! Nothing was too difficult for Him.

The worship service over, I ushered the children into the Sunday school. I loved Sunday mornings. Being surrounded by little hands, gleaming eyes and trusting smiles reinforced my need to stick to the basics – unconditional love.

Little Anna came skipping towards me holding a piece of paper that might once have been a neat little craft sheet. "Look, Ms. Jewels," she said, "my brother gave this to me." Before I could open it, she said, "This is a card from my brother. As she handed it over to me with her tiny three-year old fingers, she said, "It says he loves me very much."

I cautiously opened the piece of paper in fear of tearing it. It was in a tattered and worn envelope. There right in the middle of the colorful card was written, "Anna you are not my friend."

I avoided any sign of disappointment and gave her my best smile. Little Anna's eyes lit with joy. She took the paper and folding it in many tiny folds put it in her little purse.

She then skipped away to the playroom with gay abandon.

What bliss, innocence! At three she did not know what was written. She believed her brother loved her and nothing else mattered. Not even the fact that she was unable to read the truth!

I decided then that no matter what my brother said or did I would just love him unconditionally.

The Sunday school teacher in me had learnt a lesson that day, in unconditional love.

## Notes

_____
_____
_____
_____
_____
_____
_____
_____
_____
_____
_____
_____
_____
_____
_____
_____
_____
_____
_____
_____
_____
_____

# Chapter - 15
## The Miracle of the Empty Seat

I boarded the 747 for another grueling twelve hour journey. My first concern as always was who would be my co-passenger. As I walked to my seat, and as my eyes rested on this elderly Asian man, I felt like a deflated balloon. He looked very glum. I seemed to not exist to him. No eye contact. No acknowledgment of any sort.

I had a good co-passenger on an earlier flight so muttering thanks to God for at least that small mercy, I took my window seat, appreciating the empty center seat between us that gave me a little space to insulate me from his obviously bad mood.

This was a very full plane. Practically half of the passengers were teenagers with vivid orange, blood red and vibrant green hair – tattoos of every variety – and pierced lips, cheeks, eyebrows and tongues. I was used to the kids of the street, but my children were poor, they couldn't afford such adornment. I didn't want to judge, but it was a little unsettling. As if that wasn't enough, they spoke together all at once, everyone talking no one listening, it sounded like a gaggle of geese honking and cackling.

I strapped on my seat belt and glanced again at my co-passenger. He still looked like he was in a bad mood, even though his face was pretty expressionless. He looked as if he was in another world. We consumed our lunch in total silence. Well, I guess he wouldn't be as bad as the kids; at least he was quiet. I could take a nap.

For many long minutes, his behavior remained unchanged, still distant and unattached. As I nibbled on the cracker in my tray I smiled to myself in grim amusement. I thought he looked so cold it would snow on the equator if he landed there.

Exhausted from being almost twenty-four hours already on this journey, I decided to take advantage of the empty seat between us – the only empty seat in the whole plane!

I was recovering from a back injury. The extra seat provided some space to ease my discomfort so I tentatively used a bit of the seat to rest my legs. I didn't want to get in his "space" and make him even more upset. I curled and twisted myself trying to find some comfort, but my back was still hurting.

The old man tapped me and motioned to stretch my legs fully. He then gently covered my legs with the blanket and continued to read his book.

Through the remaining part of the journey we never spoke a word. I did not think he spoke English and I certainly did not speak Korean. But he did seem concerned about my comfort; so as the flight approached its destination, I decided to try and thank him for his kindness. To my surprise he responded. In halting English he explained to me the miracle of the empty seat.

He was a frequent flyer on Korean Air. He had earned many thousands of miles and often used it to get a vacant seat obviously for him. At that part of his disjointed narration his face which till now was somber broke into a smile and he said, "You need it more." You must understand that he had no knowledge of my back injury or the discomfort that I was suffering. Only God knew and He provided for me.

I met an angel.

So often a person's color, features or race prejudices us; sometimes it is just their mood – or what we assume is their mood.

I had learned a lesson.

Nothing is too difficult for God! His love is unconditional. His mercies are new every morning.

I curled up and went to sleep knowing I would reach my destination safely cared for by God – through a gentle and generous stranger.

## Notes

_____

_____

_____

_____

_____

_____

_____

_____

_____

_____

_____

_____

_____

_____

_____

_____

_____

_____

_____

_____

_____

_____

_____

_____

_____

# Chapter - 16

## The Miracle of the Red Blouse

The blaring of the black alarm clock broke the gentle peace of the dawn. I stretched out my hand and shut it off. Half awake, I lay in bed thinking of my most beautiful Christmas ever. I reached out and gently touched the face of the man who brought me so much joy and happiness in every way.

In the year since we had been married, we had many perfect moments and days. Life hummed with the warmth of love and care.

As I lay there I thought about the beautiful evening earlier that week with our older daughter and her husband.

We had played games, laughed, teased and exchanged gifts. It was as if time stood still. I ached for my younger daughter and her husband but they lived in another state and could not be with us that holiday.

That night I remembered that we did not pray as a family. Gently, God reminded me that that evening was an answer to prayer and the love we shared amongst us was a prayer of thanksgiving.

As we opened the presents at our own home on Christmas Eve, the magic seemed to extend. It was magical not because of the many gifts that were brought with much care and thought but because we shared the greatest gift of all – love.

I closed my eyes again and thanked God for the man who opened his heart and home to my daughters.

The alarm went off again and I got dressed to go to one of the after Christmas super sales. I had started a new business and desperately needed some new clothes. Now was a good time to get them. I pulled out my favorite red blouse and wore it over my black slacks.

I loved that blouse. It had been custom made for me in India. Besides being a perfect fit the fabric kept me warm and I thought the red brought out the colors in my eyes and hair. The red reminded me of love.

I smiled as I wore that red blouse for maybe the hundredth time. It was my favorite and I was glad no one teased me at home for wearing it so often. Slipping it on always felt like I was wrapping myself in love.

You could wear the blouse inside a jacket and it still looked good. Like love sometimes demonstrated quietly through gentle acts of kindness and mercy.

At other times I would wear the blouse with my jeans for all to see. That was like a hug or a kiss – there for someone to see and feel. All I could think was that it was one good blouse and I never needed an excuse to wear it.

I glanced in the kitchen, as I got ready to leave. Oops, there was a stain on the kitchen counter. I poured chlorine bleach onto a kitchen towel and dabbed the spot. Hurriedly, almost absent mindedly, I arranged the things in the kitchen and left.

I was half way through the shopping when I got hot and decided to remove my jacket. My daughter looked at me and exclaimed "Mom you ruined your blouse"! I looked down and to my horror and disbelief; I saw a huge pinkish-whitish spot, on my beautiful red blouse.

I almost cried. Ok, I did cry. I could never find another blouse like that again. It fit perfectly. It was custom made. I loved the color – and where was I going to get another one? This one came all the way from India. Well, if anything could mar my near perfect Christmas, it was this. I started to pray "Dear God make it not so…" Then I felt silly. Why would God care about a dumb ol' blouse? With all the problems in the world…"

Downcast, I walked to the next aisle to pick myself a pantsuit and what was that? There perched amongst all the black and blues was a red blouse. I grabbed it and held it up. It was almost identical to the one I had just ruined. I quickly tried it on and it fit me just like my old one.

The miracle lay in the realization that my blouse which I had just ruined was tailored made in India just for me and yet here I was half way round the world in a mall during an after Christmas sale, looking at a nearly identical blouse. Was it just a coincidence? I didn't think so.

I smiled as I once again remembered that He was a God of more than enough. He was also a God who cares about anything we care about. If it is important to us, it is important to Him.

The red blouse was just a gentle reminder of His great love for each of us even in the mundane hustle and bustle of everyday life.

Suddenly I felt ashamed of how I had underrated a God who had given me His all. He had given Himself.

## Notes

_____

_____

_____

_____

_____

_____

_____

_____

_____

_____

_____

_____

_____

_____

_____

_____

_____

_____

_____

_____

_____

_____

# Chapter - 17

## The Miracle of the Dancing Wheel

I have always loved Mondays. As a teenager I worked regular nine-to-five jobs and often got tired of my co-workers who complained about Mondays. Monday Blues or some other thing they called it. I decided then that I would always find something cheerful to do and would look forward to Mondays.

On one of those Mondays, which by now had become to me one of my favorite days of the week, I was driving back home from the soup kitchen where I volunteered.

Today we had about forty-five people. It was always interesting to see them, many of whom I had known for a while now and had become dear to my heart.

Old Bob was my favorite. With his full white beard and nice pot belly, he reminded me of Santa Claus. He knew it too, because every time he entered the room he just went, "Ho! Ho! Ho!" He always had gotten my mind of the fact that it was supposed to be a "Blue Monday".

Today he had me sit in front of him and relate some stories. "Tell me an interesting one," he said. So I shared with him a whole hair-raising drama about my survival on the burning airplane. Bob liked the story – and had a few funny comments about it too. After dessert he left waving and asking me to be careful on the road. Then he said, "God be with you; be blessed!"

He smiled as I waved my final goodbye and got into my car. I need to take it to the shop, since it needed some work on the wheels or tires, or something – I couldn't tell.

I got into the shop, they "fixed" it and I was on my way home or so I thought. My house was not too far from the shop. I turned and in less than three minutes on the road I saw a tire flying across the heavy traffic.

As my car suddenly started to swerve to the left, I realized that it was MY tire. All I could say was, "OH MY GOD!" – And I meant all three words of it.

In a split second I saw the tire do a beautiful dance across the highway as if it had a mind of its own. It weaved its way through the fast oncoming traffic, missed every single car in its path and landed in an empty yard, ripping the fence as it went along. In retrospect, I think I even heard it heave a sigh of relief.

Never having been in such a dilemma before, all I could do was to hit the brakes real hard to keep me from being hurled into the oncoming traffic.

The car came to screeching halt two inches from the center lane. I was still pretty dazed and taking it all in. I then realized that I could have been killed – and taken someone else with me.

I got out of the car and took note of the damage. The front end of my car was on the ground and completely trashed. I got back in the car and called my husband to come rescue me.

Was I glad that he always made sure that I carried my cell phone everywhere I went? Oh yes!

In the fifteen minutes it took him to get there I began to replay the whole scene in my head many times over. "How did the tire do such an amazing dance?" "How did my car stop just a few inches from oncoming traffic?"

Then I thought of Bob's words, "God be with you – be blessed!"

So, that was a blessing of the Lord. I realized also that there was some pretty fast angelic activity that took place there too.

Psalm 91 came to my mind, verses 11 and 12: "For He will command his angels concerning you to guard you in all your ways; they will lift you up in their hands, so that you will not strike your foot against a stone. (Nor your wheel strike an oncoming car or your face strike the dashboard – my version)."

I smiled to myself; blue Monday? Not a chance! It was now blessed Monday and would be from then on!

## Notes

_____

_____

_____

_____

_____

_____

_____

_____

_____

_____

_____

_____

_____

_____

_____

_____

_____

_____

_____

_____

_____

_____

_____

_____

# Chapter - 18

## The Miracle of the Last Gift

Suddenly my world stood at a standstill. Deafening silence, shock, and more shock. In one word: death.

My mother was gone. I was only twenty-two years old and my younger brother was seven years my junior. There was no time for tears; somehow the transition from a sister to a "mother" had to be immediate or... I had no idea and did not want to think about the possible consequences.

In those days where love marriages were not heard of in my country, my parents had a "love marriage". True to their word, my parents loved each other till death did them part.

The weeks and months ahead seemed a blur. Like walking through a fog; now you see now you don't. I don't know what I saw through my secret tears and stifled sighs, not much except a dad that needed all the help he could get and a little brother who needed all the mom he could get in me. I had to put myself on hold and probably not answer any calls from that quarter for awhile.

Being a teenager is never easy in any culture. Especially if you are headstrong and thinking way out of everything your culture teaches you with respect to little girls or even big girls. "Girls should be seen and never heard,"

Mom said. She and I often exchanged heated words about the privacy and independence I wanted.

Of course, in retrospect, I did not have to be that hot-headed. I could have talked in nicer tones and tried to understand things her way. But my hormones would have none of it. Like many of us, I would give anything to make those days better and wished that I had a better relationship with her.

It seems ages ago when she oiled and braided my long hair. I was her "Baby". She hardly called me by name except when she was really upset. Deep within, she cherished who I was and everyday gave me a feather or two so that one day when I was ready I could fly and be all that I wanted to be.

In all the busyness of life I miss her still. There is a gaping hole in my heart that no one can fill. I want to talk to her about her granddaughters. I want to tell her how beautiful they have grown to be and how much they are like her. I want to tell her all the things that I did right with them because I followed in her footsteps in so many ways. But I guess that will have to wait.

Little things I do with the girls bring her to mind. Like the time I was trying to give my eight year old a haircut. She looked at me rolled her eyes and said she wanted to go to the hairdresser. So off we went to get a professional haircut. I did not want to make her sad or feel less than the beautiful girl she was by giving her a homely hair cut.

I guess that is the reason I found those dress pants rolled in a bundle with a needle and thread still half way in a hem. Mother had not finished it. I had often wondered why. Now I thought about it once again. Why didn't she finish it? It was so unlike her.

Then all of a sudden I realized that I would never have approved of her workmanship. I would find fault. She thought I would feel sad at a job not well done and left it undone.

Over the years, the pants disappeared like so many other memories in the stream of life. What did not disappear was the fact that the unfinished business of not hemming my pants, was almost like my Mother's last gift to me. Her gift of recognizing, that I wanted to be who I was.

I began to look back over the years and counted all the feathers she had given me. "Looking back" I saw that I had a pair of well formed wings. Even when she was gone she made sure that in the years she spent raising me that there would be unseen feathers that I could cash in later on.

She believed that her "baby" would one day grow up and fly just like she had dreamed.

I thank my Mother and thank God for her, a woman of faith and utmost courage; a woman who believed in invisible wings that would make her children soar high and clear.

Thank you, Mom.

## Notes

# Chapter - 19

## The Miracle of the Bead Chain

I had just got into the Church with the idea of soaking in God's presence. Things were rough to say the least and a little respite would help. Not having had enough sleep, I began to doze off.

I did try to keep myself awake by playing "Great is Thy Faithfulness" on the church piano. I didn't get too far. By the time I reached the second verse I was falling asleep on the piano and falling off the chair.

Then I thought of sitting in the pew and reading the Bible. Just then some young men came in to fix the sound system. To make matters worse their voices droned on and on almost like a lullaby. I thought they would stop at some point of time. After about twenty minutes it still went on and I decided to leave for fear of falling asleep there.

As I took the road home, I decided to stop at the little Indian grocery store. It was always a delight to stop there and savor the smells of my homeland. My eyes on the road ahead, I started to calculate mentally what it would cost me to buy a couple of things that I needed. I almost cringed at having to spend even a dollar due to the economic situation that we were in. I decided to buy what was really essential and then get along with the rest of the day.

As I pulled up in my nice warm car in front of the store almost at the same time I saw a lady, who was perhaps in her seventies, trying to pull out an old sheet to sit on by the store on the curb side. Turning off the ignition, I sat drinking in the scene – every drop.

She was heavy set and had trouble bending and removing the sheet. She also had a couple of little bags which she was trying to arrange and rearrange. Her dress was old but clean. Her white hair almost seemed like a crown atop her little head.

I observed further her persistence in getting things done. I realized that she was in the process of setting up a little "store".  She was about to sit down when I decided to stop and say hello to her.

As she looked up, still trying to fold her sheet, I saw under the sheets a book that I have to come to revere and believe. It was an old tattered Bible. She continued with her activity. "Hi, my name is Jewels," I said as I extended my hand to shake hers. She looked up and beamed a big broad smile that added a touch of sunshine to an otherwise cloudy overcast Northwest sky.

I asked what she was doing. Smiling she said, "Oh, this little business selling beads. I want to go with my girlfriend on a short trip and am hoping to make a few dollars." She then added, "Honey, I am having trouble with my legs so I got to sit down". I asked her if she had a place to live. She replied, "Yes, don't worry about me; I am exactly where God wants me to be. He is so faithful. He loves you and me. He is wonderful and His name is Jesus".

I felt troubled. She could be my grandmother. Why was she here? Why was there no one to look after her? I knew this was a God encounter and asked if I could pray with her.

She smiled and hugged me. She held me by the waist and right there on the curbside we began to pray. Tears rolled down my cheeks unashamedly because I just felt that this was not how grammas were supposed to live.

She should be by a fireplace with a little kitten on her lap. She should have been reading a book or dozing off in between knitting a sweater for a grandchild. She should have someone to bring her a cup of hot soup and caress her worn hands. She should be bundled in warm clothes and have a nice warm bed to rest in.

I held her close to me and prayed for her through my tears. She then prayed for me and for the lady who owned the Indian store. I had been there many times but never thought of praying for the store lady. As we finished our short prayer, I knew deep within she had touched the heart of God.

She looked at me and said, still smiling, "Don't worry about me I am okay, sweetie. I am really happy about this little trip I am going on with my best friend. I am selling these little bead chains for a dollar. I really am okay. Would you like to buy one?"

How could I refuse? I bought a chain of colorful beads strung dramatically on a long nylon string.

She squeezed my hand and thanked me for buying the chain. She gave me a big bear hug and waved goodbye, still smiling.

From the time I first set my eyes on her till I left she did not stop smiling. She beamed like she had a thousand watt light bulb inside her.

I got into the car and looked at the bead chain. I thought it looked too gaudy and would give it away. Just to whom, was the question. It lay there for a couple of days till it hit me. I was going to give it to me.

Every time I would get worried about the financial situation I would look at the beads. They would remind me of a grandma whose name was Velva; who braced life not with lofty ideas and worldly knowledge but with the Word of God; who did not beat herself down for her situation and feel helpless, but rose to the occasion to do everything she could with whatever she had; still strongly relying on her faithful God.

I would remember this woman who balanced her life on the scale delicately by appropriately having faith in God for all things, yet taking action in her situation according to His leading. She had the peace that passes all understanding

Above all she was a living example of the scripture in Philippians 4:4-6:

"Rejoice in the Lord always. I will say it again: Rejoice! Let your gentleness be evident to all. The Lord is near. Do not be anxious about anything, but in everything, by prayer and petition, with thanksgiving, present your requests to God. And the peace of God, which transcends all understanding, will guard your hearts and your minds in Christ Jesus."

I met God that day; not in the sanctuary, but on the curbside. Being the loving Father that He is, He taught me a lesson in life's school in a way that I could understand.

The gaudy beads now hang in my car; a silent reminder of a lesson in faith and trust.

Great is Thy Faithfulness!

## Notes

_____

_____

_____

_____

_____

_____

_____

_____

_____

_____

_____

_____

_____

_____

_____

_____

_____

_____

_____

_____

_____

_____

_____

_____

# Chapter - 20

## The Miracle of Gratitude

"Gees!" I thought as the alarm went off, "That darn alarm – again!" I pulled the sheets closer over my ears. Still mumbling and grumbling under my breath I woke as if in a stupor and stood under the cold shower.

I dressed and went to the kitchen, popped all my pills into my mouth, held them there for a moment with a grimace before washing them all down with lukewarm tap water. They were there to keep me in good health but like many of us I never really enjoyed taking them.

I grabbed my pre-packaged boxed lunch and got into the car, crestfallen because it was going to be another day of sandwiches and yogurt.

How I wished that morning I had the luxury of this thing called time, to get a warm lunch on some days or even be able to stay home and cook a nice Indian meal.

As I got into my car I braced my self for the traffic circus. Everyone seemed always to be in a hurry and impatient. A driver cut in front of me. I rolled my eyes and tried to keep my inner peace.

Later in the evening that day I learned a much deserved lesson.

It was a cold night and about eight of us were at a park helping an organization distribute small packaged dinners to the homeless.

As I joined the group, we laid out the food and got some coffee percolating. The aroma of the fresh coffee was a siren's call and people began to arrive to get their share of the simple meal of hot dogs and chips. There were men, few women and children too.

As I glanced down the line my eyes rested on a fragile old man, close to the end of the line, waiting to be served. He must have been seventy years old – maybe older. I did not know his story. I didn't need to. It was all there, written on his face for every one to see. Lines deepened by years of sadness and lack; wrinkles left there by years of exposure to the harsh winds of poverty, despair – and perhaps children or grandchildren who did not care.

"How are you"? I asked.

"Good," he replied, "Nothing to complain about Ma'am, nothing to complain about." He took the bag of chips I handed him and with a gracious bow of his head moved on ahead to get his hot dog. As he passed, a smile flickered on his lips, giving him for a moment, an angelic appearance. I watched him intensely, feeling a strange mixture of sorrow and gratitude.

Nothing to complain about? His clothes were in tatters; shoes full of holes. His threadbare gloves must have been retrieved from a dumpster. His back was bent as if under the weight of years of struggle. Someone's once beloved husband maybe, someone's precious father... who knows?

I would be soon going home to a warm bed and a hot cup of apple cider. Dinner would be ready and I would enjoy the warmth of people who loved me. I had a family, the greatest gift of all.

My feet were nestled in warm furry winter shoes; my hands toasty inside new gloves; my ears protected from the icy cold winds by a bright red woolen cap. I had always been well clothed and always provided for. I could talk, hear, see, walk and run. My back was still straight.

Suddenly I had nothing to complain about. From that day forth, I would be more careful to count my blessings!

## Notes

_____

_____

_____

_____

_____

_____

_____

_____

_____

_____

_____

_____

_____

_____

_____

_____

_____

_____

_____

_____

_____

_____

_____

_____

_____

# Chapter - 21
## *The Miracle of a No Tears Day*

Our home was always a busy place. The buzz of activity came from over eight or nine uncles and aunts who visited us very weekend. My parents, Maggie and Joseph, did not talk about hospitality, but quietly lived the way they knew best.

Each of my uncles and aunts were new to the city. They came from a distant village in South India. Having finished their degrees there weren't any jobs available in a place that was primarily agricultural, so just naturally they headed to over to Maggie's house.

My parents had come to Bombay years before and were well settled, according to the village grapevine.

The reality was that only my dad worked. My dear mother was a great homemaker and sacrificed many things just to be with her children. So, between two adults and three growing children, there wasn't anything much left at the end of the month except a lot of patience and raised eyebrows.

Dad came from the northern part of India and mother from the southern end.

They had totally different cultures and traditions. You have to visit India and live there for at least a year to understand that. The diversity is as stark as night and day. We were children of the "third culture."

Growing up was wonderful. My parents were wonderful disciplinarians though they never even saw a page of a book on parenting. Their consistency in discipline laid a strong foundation in our lives.

Their acceptance of our different personalities and their ability to make each child feel favored and special was indeed commendable. That was before laws for spanking were part of any constitution.

This is a true story of a lady who never bought us any presents all our lives. Every special occasion was celebrated with a wonderful lunch and a great dinner. Times were hard.

As I mentioned earlier my Dad was the only wage-earning member of the family and he had to feed, clothe, and educate my two brothers and me. So presents were out – but family times were in. So were lots of hugging and tickling and slurpy kisses.

As I was growing up, I noticed a rare gift that my mother gave to us on every birthday, Easter, Christmas and New Year. In her heart and mind she had decided that because she could not gift us any material thing she would make it a "No Tears" day.

Consistently as I was growing up I tested this. Having celebrated my sixteenth birthday in November I decided to have a memorable glamour shot taken on Christmas! Oh, the days of vain "teenage-hood".

I had tried asking her for the money in between my birthday on fifteenth November, and twenty-fourth December and the answer was always a flat, "no". But when I asked her on the twenty-fifth of December she opened her little purse and handed me the money for the snap shot.

Another time I wanted to join swimming lessons. I have always enjoyed the rainy season and was adamant on taking swimming lessons in the monsoons that was in the month of July. As I mentioned earlier, things were difficult, financially and to get some money out of my mom for swimming lessons was a challenge.

From July to November thirteenth I kept asking her for the money and always the answer was, "Not now, I am really strapped for cash."

Then came my birthday and that morning as my mother kissed me "Happy Birthday" my first request was, "Mom, can I have swimming lessons?" Without a protest she opened the cupboard and handed me the money.

I know things were as difficult now as they were in July. But somehow it seemed that she had the miracle of bestowing an extra smile and a glad heart on her children on those special days.

Now I have my own family. Financially, I am doing a lot better than my parents. There are always gifts on birthdays, a movie, a party, a new dress sometimes a couple of new dresses but over and above all, I make it a point to see that it's a "No Tears" day.

What a beautiful legacy my mom left me. Not one that money can buy but just one with a mind that was extra thoughtful and a heart that was
extra loving.

## Notes

# Chapter - 22

## *The Miracle of Shanky*

It seemed like just another sunny day. On my schedule again was to find children that were abandoned and then take them "home". Sometimes they would come trustingly. Other times they would just talk a little and then melt into the crowd.

As I scouted the busy railway station, my eyes fell on a little guy about five years old. I noticed that his hair stood like stalks of pollen growing in all different directions. Head bowed, he stood in a corner by the railway stairs. His clothes were tattered and it looked as if he had not had a shower or a bath for a few weeks.

My heart went out to him. I walked towards him and tousled his hair and smiled. He peered at me ever so gently from the corner of his eye letting me take his hand. So tiny, so helpless and yet it seemed like some unseen survival kit placed inside him had kept him alive all these years.

I asked him if he would like to have a cup of tea and a sandwich. He gladly agreed. We sat and talked for awhile. His mother had abandoned him when he was a toddler. His father died when he was about three years old and left him in the care of a cruel uncle. He managed to find a friend in a ten year old cousin and they ran away from what was supposed to be their only home.

As he reached out for the sandwich, I saw a scar on his hand. On inquiring he said that his uncle use to burn him with cigarette butts whenever he was upset with him and then hang him upside down. I was appalled but it was not unusual to hear such stories. I felt the urgency to take him home.

I patted his hand and then held him close. Shanky just smiled and kept wolfing the sandwich down. After we finished, he decided he did not want to come home with me but would continue to live at the railway station.

**Mommy and Shanky**

Every few days I would go look for him. I prayed constantly that he would have wisdom to get off the streets. My job was to build trust and let him know that I loved him unconditionally.

Every visit was almost sacred. Forging a bond with an abused child who was never loved and abandoned at such a tender age was not easy but I was determined to win him over.

Umpteen visits and eighteen months later, he decided I was good enough for him. He put his hand in mine and we walked home together to a future of love and hope.

Bathing, scrubbing, laughing, talking, dreaming, bed-time stories and many unshed and shed tears later our lives merged as two sweet fragrances in one family. He became a part of our lives and everyone simply loved him.

Shanky's presence in our lives was like the dreamy fragrance of honeysuckles that woke us every morning. Woke us to a day filled with hugs, kisses and laughter. Shanky had a great sense of humor and was always up to something funny. He often would come to me with a serious face and have me all worried. Then he would break into giggles when I would realize it was just another of his silly tricks.

He was also a child with a very caring heart. Once I asked all the boys to pray for a particular problem that we were all facing. A few weeks later the problem got solved. The older kids knew about it and somehow everyone forgot to tell Shanky. Three months down the road Shanky came to me and asked me if I had an answer to that prayer. I looked puzzled and then realized he was still praying for the problem to be solved. He was a special child.

In a few years Shanky made great strides. Today the sun shines bright on the doorstep of Shanky's future, removing shadows of long standing ailments and illiteracy. He is a young man full of hope and with a bright future.

## Notes

_____

_____

_____

_____

_____

_____

_____

_____

_____

_____

_____

_____

_____

_____

_____

_____

_____

_____

_____

_____

_____

_____

_____

# Chapter - 23

## The Miracle of the Misaddressed Letter

The ocean waves seem to run towards me to kiss my feet. I loved the beach, the warm water and the sunsets as far as I could remember. Life was beautiful for me when I was a child.

I was blessed with wonderful parents. The only thing I had to worry about was getting good grades. My dad always made me feel like the world belonged to me. I was his little princess. If ever there was a daddy's little girl, it was me.

That was twenty-eight years ago. I was all grown up now; busy taking care of two little girls of my own. They were my world. As the waves touched my feet, I remembered I had to get going. It would be dark soon and my friend Suzanna, who had my children for the day, was going stop by to drop them off. Her husband, William was going to then take all of us out for some ice-cream.

As I walked home, I thought of another William I knew as a little girl. He was a distant relative. His mother died when he was about five. Larry, his dad, had decided never to marry again in the fear that he might not find the perfect mother for his dear son.

My parents were good friends with his dad. William studied in a boarding school and visited us on weekends. We were the only family he had.

My mother loved this little boy and he felt at home with us. So now, instead of just two brothers, I had three. He often bullied me and said, "I am your big brother, obey me." I smiled as I remembered his fake deep voice.

The four of us often did things together. Time flew by and we were soon all close to graduating from school. That year I had needlework as a subject and had spent painstaking hours finishing my project.

When it was finally done I heaved a sigh of relief. Mother thought that my work was really praiseworthy. It was a pillow cover (sham) with beautiful roses, daises and butterflies. After I got graded for my work, I wanted to give that to my mother.

I picked up the pillow cover a couple of times during the day admiring my work and how I had finally got it done. Phew! That to me was incredible, as I really did not like needlework.

I heard the door bell ring and ran to open the door. My friend Tessie was there. We had decided to go to the local library to pick some books. I threw the pillow cover on the couch and left.

After having spent some time in the library we headed home. I looked at the time and remembered that William would be home today. He was older now and sometimes would come by himself. Larry was getting on in years and liked spending time with his old buddies.

I walked in and to my horror William was holding my project in his hands and it was completely undone. He had as painstakingly removed every stitch as I had painstakingly done it.

I was appalled. I burst into tears and fled in my room. I wept for hours. I felt betrayed. I was angry and even worse; I had to re-do the project within forty-eight hours, almost an impossible task. "How could he do this to me?" He was my "brother". He knew I hated needlework. I sobbed all evening and fell asleep.

William was gone the next morning. He had a hockey match in school. I decided then that I was never going to talk to him again. I kept my decision. He came a few weeks later. I ignored him. Then a few weeks later I ignored him again and made him feel unwelcome. I kept doing this until he stopped coming.

My mother tried to speak sense to me; tried to get me to forgive him. "It is only a project. William is family." I ignored her words. Somehow when you are a haughty teenager everything seems so right, your way.

That was the last I saw of William for a long time.

I began to climb that little hill that would take me back to the road from the beach. I looked up and could see the stars. I just realized how long I had carried unforgiveness in my heart, for a childhood prank – almost ten years now.

Suddenly I started to weep. I began to feel William's pain at being rejected. What a fool I had been. Would I ever have a chance to find him and ask him to forgive me? I had lost track of William. He had moved on to another suburb and I had no idea where he lived or what he did. I bowed my head in prayer, "Lord, find William for me so I can ask him to forgive me."

A week later I had a letter in the mail from a bank telling me that a check in my favor had been wrongly directed to their bank. They also asked me to come with my identification papers and pick it up. I decided to go the next day and clear the matter.

I reached the bank in a high rise building in Bombay city at about noon. There did not seem to be a reception area so I walked into the office to find where I could pick my check up.

As I was taking to the gentleman behind the desk I heard the tap of a pencil next to me on the table. I looked up and to my utter disbelief, it was William.

It had been ten long years but he hadn't changed much. He smiled as if nothing had ever gone wrong between us and said, "What brings you here?" I quickly explained the situation and asked him if he would walk me outside.

He then said that was not his office cubicle. His was way on the other side and he had come to drop off some papers at this end. He smiled and said he would wait till I got done.

I walked outside with William escorting me. As we reached outside I looked at him and tears began to flow. "William, can you forgive me? I am so sorry. I was young and stupid. It was all a horrible mistake; sorry, William, sorry."

He gently squeezed my hand and said, "I forgive you; I am your big brother, remember?" He then smiled and the world seemed brighter and my load lighter.

As I crept into bed that night I could hear the waves gently lapping the shore. I began to go over the days events. I had learned a few lessons that day. It was easier to forgive because a loving God had forgiven me.

I learned that God was intricately involved with every detail of my life. I learned that it was a not coincidence for me to find William, in a city of twelve million people. Without a doubt it was an answer to prayer and a "God-incidence".

# *Notes*

# Chapter - 24

## *The Miracle of the Last Ride*

I glanced at my watch and saw that I had just enough time to cross over the railway bridge and start school. The children would always be there before me, anxious to get started. They would wait for me to come with the books and breakfast. It was a great combination. I was running through the list of things to do in my head.

Sunny needed to see a dentist. Raja needed to visit the local clinic for an injured toe which was not healing very well. Sasha needed to get her tuberculosis medicine. She was just nine and had already been hit with the disease – but it was curable as long as she took her medicine. The list went on and on.

Street children were not a priority with the government or local authorities so it was always a hassle to get any kind of proper aid. Until that help came, I decided we could get along with the program. Today there were about forty-five children. School was a couple of little mats laid out on the ground. The number of children varied on whether they had to go beg or were traveling with a parent to some other railway station.

Having finished school for the day and sorted most of the problems out, I headed back to the west side of the bridge to go home.

As I rushed out of the crowded railway station, I almost tripped over the body of a man lying right under the last step at the exit gate of the railway station.

I stopped and looked. He seemed to be about eighty years old and appeared to be dying. He had black and blue bruises all over his arms. Someone had apparently beaten him and left him there to die.

Since he was sprawled by a little tea stall, I asked the stall owner if he knew anything. "No", he replied. "I got here this morning and the man was already lying here when I arrived." Nonchalantly he just went back to his work.

I stood there for a few minutes and took in the scene. People were passing by without really looking at him. Some threw a coin or two at him as if he could get up and run to the store to buy food and bandages. I did understand, somewhat. Every day there were hundreds of people on the streets that needed some kind of help. The office goers were just too busy and got used to doing their bit even if it was totally ineffective. I guess it kind of soothed their soul.

I decided I had to do something different. There was no 911 to call; nor was there an ambulance service. I did call up a couple of hospitals and nobody seemed interested in coming out to get him. So I decided to take him to a shelter.

One of the street kids passing by asked if he could help. Then I remembered one of our volunteers was a tall guy who could help. So I asked him to tell Austin that I needed his help.

Austin arrived a few minutes later, looked at the man, looked at me and of course deemed that I was completely crazy to be trying to help. He looked bewildered and I don't blame him because there wasn't an ambulance in sight.

Outside all railway stations you can find something called a 'rickshaw'. They are the answer to cheap cabs. A little scooter that has its side covered to comfortably seat three people. Seating three people would be a challenge because this old man was not capable of sitting. He seemed almost dead and needed to be in a lying down position.

A rickshaw on the busy streets of Bombay

So I asked the first rickshaw driver. After learning what I had to do, he simply said, "No," and drove away. So also did the second, the third, and the fourth; they all just drove away as soon as they realized why I wanted their help – even though I offered to pay, it was apparently just too much trouble. After fifteen precious minutes and nearly ten rickshaws I decided I had to stop being so nice.

The next rickshaw that stopped I stood in front of it. Then I started to talk to the driver I told him why I needed his services and that someday it could be his father in the same position or worse; maybe some day, God forbid, it could be him. I managed to guilt him into giving us a ride to the shelter that was forty-five minutes away.

I got in first, and then Austin picked the man and laid his head on my lap. Austin now got in and gently held the man's legs so that he would not roll over. The journey began.

The road to the shelter was full of potholes. It was on the outskirts of the city and so no one really cared about the roads here. We had to hold on to dear life – both this frail old man's and ours.

I gave him a little water and then gently stroked his forehead. The old man smiled faintly and then a teardrop fell. Austin continued to hold his hand. Then I asked him what his name was.

He opened his mouth to reply and then there was silence. His head fell to the side and so did his arm. Austin and I looked in utter disbelief at each other. He was dead.

Without a word, we continued to the shelter. When we got there, we gently took him out and laid him in the foyer. A volunteer from the shelter came out and examined him.

"Hmmm…he said, "No pulse. Can you guys wait here and fill out the paper work for his last rites? You would have to put yourself as next of kin."

The papers were brought and I signed them. Was I his next of kin? No, but he was my fellow countryman. He was someone's dad, someone's brother; he was a human being who should be buried with dignity.

We shared the same Father. He was my brother, I guess then I was his kin.

As I walked away from the shelter to the waiting rickshaw to take me back, I held back my tears and began to thank God for the opportunity of being able to comfort one of His children during his last moments on earth.

My mind went to a scripture verse I read that morning:

"Whatsoever you do to the least of my brothers; you do unto me. For when I was hungry you gave me something to eat, I was thirsty and you gave me something to drink, I was a stranger and you invited me in, I needed clothes and you clothed me, I was sick and you looked after me, I was in prison and you came to visit me."

I was dying and you cared enough to love.

## Notes

_____

_____

_____

_____

_____

_____

_____

_____

_____

_____

_____

_____

_____

_____

_____

_____

_____

_____

_____

_____

_____

_____

_____

_____

_____

_____

# Chapter - 25
## The Miracle of the Shoelace

The cool monsoon breeze wafted in carrying the smell of the roses outside my window. I took a deep breath. The rains had cleaned the city for whatever it was worth! I looked out and caught a glimpse of the sun smiling behind the now grayish clouds. I then glanced at my tennis shoes. They were stained from the mud and rain. It was time to get a new pair.

I quickly picked up my handbag and was about to dash out of the door. I remembered I would need a large napkin to hold over my nose as I made my way through the city streets. The fumes from the overcrowded city made me sick. I often felt like I was locked in a gas chamber. Knowing that I was in the city with a divine purpose, I smiled. I knew that God had called me to minister in this city would take care of me.

I entered the busy shop and picked the sandals I thought were most comfortable.

I threw a glance at my watch, realizing that I had to hurry back to go to the doctor. It was six-thirty and my appointment was at seven-thirty. Just enough time to get back.

Alighting from the rickshaw, I hurriedly crossed the street. A few minutes later I was inside the clinic. Having an appointment helped. The doctor gave me some medication for a week to help with my immune system to combat the pollution. Alternative medicines had their advantage!

Now it was time to go back home. I picked up my belongings. The old shoes now quietly lay in the plastic bag. As I stepped out of the clinic and onto the sidewalk my eyes grew large in horror. What I saw was beyond my wildest imagination.

Right there in front of me was a man who was bleeding profusely from his forearm. I quickly took in his appearance. He was about twenty-five or so. Disheveled, and drunk. Blood was gushing in spouts and he was in a state of shock. Here, there was no 911!

I began to pray frantically as people just passed by not wanting to be involved. Within minutes people were gathered around. In his rasping voice the man weakly narrated his story about his lover who jilted him. There was no time to hear more. He had to be saved!

Someone asked if anyone had a napkin or a towel. There was no clinic near by and the nearest Government hospital was about three miles away! I remembered the napkin and pulled it out of my bag. I handed it to the burly man who was trying to help the injured man. Then a voice from the small crowd said, "Get a rope so we can tie a tourniquet", some of them just ran hither thither to find it. The man continued to bleed looking more and more ghastly with each passing second.

I again began to frantically look inside my bag. "Lord", I prayed, "help me"! Just then the white shoelaces caught my attention. I quickly drew them out of the shoes and handed it over to the Good Samaritan. Not worrying about any infection, or ignorant of the possibility of the same, he tied the tourniquet.

Finally, help came in the form of an old man. He stopped his car and offered to take the young man to the Government hospital. I slowly backed away from the crowd.

No one noticed me leave. I smiled to myself. I knew he would be okay. I knew that the man who tried to stop the bleeding with his bare hands would be okay. I knew that the old man would be okay. Somehow I knew that in the final equation a good God would make it all okay.

## Notes

_____

_____

_____

_____

_____

_____

_____

_____

_____

_____

_____

_____

_____

_____

_____

_____

_____

_____

_____

_____

_____

_____

_____

_____

_____

# Chapter - 26

## The Miracle of a Silent Love

I was all of nineteen and thought I could do just about anything. So when I learned that there was a job at the school for the visually impaired, I was all ready to take it.

As I walked into the Principal's office she looked at me with a slight frown. I was a frail young girl, five feet four inches tall, hair neatly braided and wearing a fluorescent green dress with socks and tennis shoes! Little did I know that was not the way to dress for an interview.

She asked me to sit as she looked over my resume. It really wasn't much. All I had done in the last year was attend college. I had still three more years to finish my degree. Then she looked at me real hard and said, "What can you do?" I somehow knew it was a moment to make it or break it. Mustering all my courage and keeping a brave front belying my nervous inner tumult I said, "Give me a chance and I can really do this." She talked with me some more and then I was on my way.

For three days I waited for a letter in the mail addressed to me from the school. Finally it came and I tore the envelope open; almost ripping the letter in the process. "You have been selected for the job. Please report Monday morning... " The rest was a blur.

I was off on a challenge that I had bargained for. I was just nineteen and had been selected to work as a teacher in a school for the visually impaired. There would be a six month training period and I would be a regular teacher.

School like most other things in life was a challenge. I loved the little boys and we did have a lot of fun. It was amazing to see how their sense of hearing was keenly developed.

Their musical skills were astounding. I came to learn from them that there were really no "disabilities" if one was determined to be successful.

Although the school had been established in 1925, the pre-vocational training began only twenty-five years ago. There were four areas into which the children (with little or no vision) were absorbed: pottery, carpentry, handloom and the most recent addition, mosaic.

Jim was severely visually impaired. He made crucifixes by hand, using only his fingers to mould. "I felt the crucifix which I have at home and understood the shape. I don't take time to create, just one class and the crucifix is ready," he smiled and said.

Likewise, Mohammed, Subhash and Rajesh worked on mosaic designs for trays and table tops. With only partial eyesight, they painstakingly picked up pieces of cut-glass and stuck them onto acrylic sheets to create patterns.

Mosaic was a recent addition in the school. It began as an experiment and now, after much trial and error, the children created the most wonderful mosaic designs in vivid colors.

They learned to work with precision techniques by carefully cutting the glass and then reconstructing it in a specific way that preserved the look. They seem to have magic in their finger tips.

Many of the children came from far off villages since they were really the ones whose sights were affected due to poor nutrition. They lived in the school and it was a home away from home.

I was a fifth grade class teacher. Thirty boys in a class were quite a handful. They were always eager to learn and eager to please. I loved each one of them dearly.

Sometimes we would play catch. The ball had some bells inside it and when it was rolled, they would follow the sound and catch it. They never behaved like they had a handicap. They laughed, played and loved just like any other children.

I had seen children accidentally bump into each other and laugh. I had seen them accidentally trip over one another and laugh but then I saw anger because of some intentional cruel thing that was said or done. They had it all figured out, I thought, at a tender age.

One more day being over, I waved good-bye to the boys and ran toward the bus stop that was just outside the school. My cousin Laurie, who I had not seen in many years, was coming to visit me. I was excited she was about the same age as me and we shared common interests.

All the way home I kept thinking about her. As little girls we played "house". As we grew older, we talked about tests and movies.

I was sure this week we would go to a certain movie I had wanted to see for awhile. When I got home Laurie was already there. We hugged and kissed and talked for awhile. Late that night we started talking about what we would do the next day. Of course we both already knew what we were going to do; we were going to the movies!

Then we started to discuss which movie. I wanted to go for the one I had made up my mind about and Laurie wanted to see something else. After half hour deliberation, we both refused to give in and went to bed angry.

I got up the next morning and left for school. Laurie always had her way as a little girl. She cried and whined as far back as I could remember to have things her way. Not this time, I thought to myself. I was determined it was either my way or no way.

She would be gone tomorrow and that would be the end of it.

As I walked into my classroom I was surprised to see the Principal there. She asked me to take the first graders today as their teacher was sick.

My students would be sent to an extra music class, they would be taken care of.

This was going to be different. I did know some of the little ones, since their class was just next to the library. I ran down the short flight of stairs, excited to be doing something new today, teaching something different.

Little did I know that I was going to attend one of life's most poignant lessons; a lesson I would never forget.

I went around meeting all the little ones. Some were painfully shy; others bold. I decided to warm the day with a little sing-song. Just then someone knocked on the door.

On opening I saw Mrs. Desai with her little son. I had met Kenny before he was about five, an adorable handsome little boy with deep dimples in his cheeks. He was extremely shy. Whenever he smiled, his dimples would just get deeper.

Today she had brought along her other son too. She introduced him to me as her little Sam. He seemed completely normal, 'til they had to say their goodbyes.

Sam stepped forward and touched Kenny on his cheeks. Kenny was visually impaired and he needed to know that Sam was leaving. Then instead of just saying, "Bye," Kenny leaned forward felt Sam's face and kissed him. Then they both hugged each other for a few moments. Mrs. Desai leaned over and looking directly at Sam, signed him that they had to leave.

He nodded kissed his brother again and squeezed his hand. I watched in disbelief and then Mrs. Desai looked at me and said, "Yes, what you see is true, Kenny cannot see and Sam is deaf and dumb. This is how they show their love to one another."

Mrs. Desai was well versed with the sorrows of life and I think at some moment in her life had decided to make the best of what she had.

As she left I took Kenny by the hand and sat him in his chair. I started the sing song once again.

As I boarded the bus that evening I decided we would go for the movie that Laurie wanted to see.

In that classroom two little boys quite innocently taught me the language of love.

## Notes

_____

_____

_____

_____

_____

_____

_____

_____

_____

_____

_____

_____

_____

_____

_____

_____

_____

_____

_____

_____

_____

_____

_____

# Chapter - 27

## *The Miracle of the Visitation*

Pete is still not doing very well. He is still in the I.C.U. His condition quite serious today. I came home because there is no sense in staying there; they don't let you in the I.C.U anyway. The lobby is full of families of accident victims constantly being brought in. It is distressing to say the least. It is hard being all by myself. Wish you were all here. Anyway, I will keep you informed. Pete may still make it and come out of this well. It is sad because he is such a good man and loves me like a dream. It was a great first year of our married life. I am truly married to the best man a woman could ever find.

My happiness was always the uppermost in his mind and he always treated me as his equal. He made sure that I was smiling and laughing he would have it no other way. It's sad to see him so helpless and lying in bed in so much pain. Well, life has many twists and turns and I am thankful for the life that he and I shared. All I can do is hope and pray that we have more healthy and happy days ahead.

I am not angry at God. In fact this will make my faith stronger; for it is not God's will that we suffer, nor did God make Pete sick. Jesus died in Pete's place. The Bible says that by the stripes and wounds of Jesus we are healed. Sometimes healing may come in ways that we do not expect.

I thank God for such a wonderful brother like you. Wish you were not all the way in India right now. Lots of friends here have risen to the occasion to help in anyway they can. That is a great thing to see, the beauty of pure love and deep compassion.

As you know, last May God laid on my heart to start a soup kitchen in the city centre on Mondays. Last Sunday when some of homeless folks went to another place to eat they put in a prayer request for Pete. It is amazing to see those that have so many needs but put the needs of others before their own. I am blessed.

I can sit and count the volume of the tragedy or I can focus on God's many blessings and I am choosing to do the later.

Love you and just had to share this little bit.

Take care now and talk to you or email you soon.

Love hugs and kiss

Jewels

I pressed the "send" button on that letter and a few minutes later was boarding the bus to go see my husband in the hospital. On the 12$^{th}$ of January 2004 he had an aneurysm burst at the nape of his neck. It was almost sixteen hours by the time he got any medical aid. It was as if yesterday I could feel the comforting arm of the neurosurgeon on my back and his gentle voice saying, "Mrs. Mesaros there is no medical explanation as to why your husband is alive. He should have died the moment the aneurysm burst. We will try all we can to save him."

That was almost four weeks ago and still there was no sign of any improvement. If there was any sign, it was just that his condition kept getting worse and worse. I remember it was a Sunday almost four weeks into the unfortunate incident.

I was at my wits end. I had prayed every prayer I knew how. I had cried till I thought I had no more tears. That morning at a friend's church I lay prostrate before the altar asking God to give me strength through the dark night of the soul and to restore my dear husband.

After the service my friend dropped me at the hospital. As I walked into Pete's room he was listless. I looked at him; it was too many weeks too long. I knew the doctor's were almost feeling helpless. Whenever I would ask them his condition they would say, "It all can change from hour to hour."

Feeling completely drained and utterly hopeless I decided to go out for a bit of fresh air.

I had no one to turn to that day. I decided to go into McDonald's and have a drink. I sat there sipping my lemon aid but my tears would not stop. They seem to arise from some deep unstoppable reservoir within my heart.

All of sudden two men walked up to me, the older one looked me straight in the eye and said, "Why are you crying?" I haltingly through my tears told him about Pete, how sick he was and how he may never get well.

Then in a warm gentle voice he said, "Look at me, I want you to believe that Pete is going to get well," and he added, "Remember, there are two men walking this city praying for his recovery. You will have him back."

With that they both smiled and left. I realized that they did not get anything to eat and were there in that place as if on a mission.

That evening a couple of friends came in and prayed for Pete. When I left that night Pete was still in serious condition. I slept by the phone all night wondering what news it would bring when it rang.

I was up at the crack of dawn and headed straight for the hospital. Of course I expected to see Pete still laying down in serious condition. As I half ran and half walked into his room he was sitting and smiling.

The team of doctors just came in that time, looked him over checked his paper work and the same neurosurgeon who had talked with me about four weeks ago said, "Mrs. Mesaros looks like he has turned the corner".

Orders were given immediately for him to be shifted out of the I.C.U.

Often times when things look hopeless I remember the two men that walked the streets praying for a heartbroken princess to have her prince back.

Within less than a month Pete was stable and well on his way to recovery. Very few people survive brain aneurysms and very few come away without disabilities. Pete did.

Angels? Without a doubt!

## Notes

_____
_____
_____
_____
_____
_____
_____
_____
_____
_____
_____
_____
_____
_____
_____
_____
_____
_____
_____
_____
_____
_____
_____

# Chapter - 28

## The Miracle of Venus

Her tiny little frame had gotten smaller in the past three weeks. Venus was just six years old and beset with an unknown illness.

I looked with anguish at my baby. She had lost about six pounds in a month and was almost skeletal. Her stomach would bloat excessively after she would eat anything even a miserly cookie and then when the bloating would become unbearable she would throw up. This went on for almost two months.

That evening I prepared to go back to the pediatrician for one more report. As I opened the door to his office, he looked real somber and said, "Jewels, we will have to conduct some more tests, this does not look good."

He then called his assistant and asked her to fix some appointments at the local hospital for further tests. He said he could not give Venus any medicines as he was still unsure what the problem was.

I picked up my little girl and walked out of the clinic fighting back tears. I hugged her real tight and kissed her soft cheek. My girls were my life's treasures.

It seemed just yesterday that they had stepped into the world. Now Venus was all of six and Neptune four years old. The girls were always full of giggles and ceaseless chatter.

But today Venus was quiet all the way home. I got home and tucked her into bed. Dinner was not an option. She just could not keep anything down.

I stayed up for a bit playing with Neptune and soon she was tired from a long day of staying with friends.

Having both in bed was a relief. Now I could take care of some things. I knelt down by the bedside and began to talk to God. "God", I pled, "please heal my girl. I am tired and she is tired, we are at the end of our rope. It is really horrible to see her suffer like this. Heal my girl, Lord, please heal my girl."

Then in the quiet of the night I heard Him say loud and clear to me, "Jewels, to whom you belong?"

I thought to myself, "Why does He ask me that? He knows I belong to Him.

I whispered, "You died in my place Lord, paid for my sins, You redeemed me and sealed me for heaven by the sacrifice on the cross. I am already completely sold out and radical for You".

Then I heard Him ask me again, "To whom, then, does everything you have belong?"

I quickly answered, "To you Lord."

Then as sure as I know my name He asked me, "To whom does Venus belong?"

I answered, "To you."

Then He said to me almost in a whisper, "Can you give her up to me, to do as I please?"

For a moment a chill ran down my spine. Now I was bawling and sobbing, "My little girl, give her away?" Then I began to meditate for a brief deep moment what His love meant. He gave Himself for me that I might have life. He loved me dearly enough to die for me. Still sobbing I opened my clenched fists and asked Him to take it all.

I don't know when I fell asleep that night. I woke up to the chirping of birds and looked mortified at the alarm clock. I had fifteen minutes to dress and get Venus ready to go downtown where another test was scheduled.

As I rushed and scurried to dress I noticed that Venus was fast asleep. She had not woken even once during the night. Since she had fallen ill, neither she nor I had a good night's rest. I tiptoed closer and checked that her chest was moving and there was warm breath in her tiny nostrils.

I decided to cancel the test and just wait at home. It was rare to see her so sound asleep and I thought that would do her some good. I glanced at my watch; it was five in the morning.

My heart was searching the heavens and hoping for a miracle. I sat down in the recliner and began to think about life and its many gifts.

As I sat drinking in the quiet morning, I opened my journal and read what I written a few months ago.

"Venus and Neptune are not just dreams and planets. You can't kiss dreams and planets. They are God's dreams and ideas translated into flesh and blood.

Their first full throated cry is now replaced by quivered smiles like satin moonbeams, sifting through mysterious woods. Nothing can change the fact that they are my own. Yet change is inevitable. As mother and children we will grow apart. Their strong wings and dreams woven with neon lights in still dark nights will take them further than I can imagine."

Suddenly I heard the patter of feet in the hallway and before I could get up Venus came running into my arms and screamed, "Mom, I am healed"!

She laughed and did a little dance. I hugged her. There was no reason for unbelief. Looking at her countenance I knew she was healed.

I held her close to me and heaved a deep sigh of relief. My Lord gave my gift back to me.

Excitedly I called the doctor and told him that Venus was healed. There was a brief silence and then he said, "In twelve years in my practice as a pediatrician I have never heard anything like this." He asked me if I could bring her back to the clinic in a couple of days for a checkup.

Venus completely recovered. She was not on any medication during that time as they were unable to diagnose her case. She is now all of twenty-six, married to Eldon, who is a great guy. She is studying to someday open her own Montessori school. She is a much loved teacher, a great writer and a wonderful daughter.

These gifts are becoming more and more exquisite and complex as time goes by. Exquisite, complex, individualistic and yet through space and galaxies intrinsically woven together by a simple term "miracle of my womb".

## Notes

_____

_____

_____

_____

_____

_____

_____

_____

_____

_____

_____

_____

_____

_____

_____

_____

_____

_____

_____

_____

_____

_____

_____

_____

_____

# Chapter - 29

## *The Miracle of Neptune*

My excitement knew no bounds when I realized that I was going to be the mother of another little girl. I had no sisters and my own mother had passed away a few years ago.

Though in my culture it was not the "in thing" to want a girl, I prayed fervently for another little girl. It had been a long nine months. Like most pregnancies it was riddled with its share of morning sickness which, fortunately, did not last the whole term.

A few months ago, we had moved into a developing suburb. Our home was located in an area that had new roads that were still being built.

There were not many condominiums around and most of the area was underdeveloped and marshy. No cab driver ever wanted to venture out there. We did not own a car and so life was going to be a challenge where travel was concerned.

I was registered at a hospital that was about an hour and half away. With no transportation and no help it was going to be a real test of faith if I had to go the hospital at midnight.

Dad was too old to take on the responsibility of me having to live with him. He lived closer to the hospital where I was to give birth.

The next few months passed by quickly. Setting up house and trying to make it nice and livable for the new baby on her way.

It was    January 28, 1982. Late in the night, as I just finished dinner and was preparing to do the dishes, I began to get mild contractions.

I looked at the clock on the wall, it was close to midnight. For a moment fear gripped me and I realized that I was alone in my new house and practically cut off from civilization.

We did not even have a telephone. Not in a million years did I think that I would have to go to the hospital in the middle of the night.

I stood still and prayed. Just then I thought about a cab that I had seen a couple of times parked in the next condominium complex.

Wearing my slippers I walked in the still of the night to the next complex which was about two-hundred yards away. Entering the gate I asked the security man who owned the cab. He pointed out to the fifth floor. My heart sank. I would have to climb at least over a hundred steps to get there.

I looked at the light in the window beckoning me bringing hope in a time of fear and distress.

Gingerly I began the climb.  Reaching the top floor I knocked gently on the door. It was opened by an elderly lady. I quickly told her my story. She looked at me in disbelief and said, "Yes, my son owns the cab and he just got back home from work. Actually it is a miracle that he is home early and I am sure he will take you to the hospital."

She also added that he was getting ready to have his dinner. Having overheard our conversation he came to the door and ushered me outside. Two complete strangers suddenly were partaking in the miracle of a new life.

He gently helped me down the long flight of stairs. For some strange reason I was not having any contractions. That was a blessing as I would never have been able to climb up and down the numerous steps.

Picking my bags, I got in the cab. Earlier, I had left Venus at my Dad's house and continued on the journey to a new chapter in my life. We drove in silence to the hospital. For some reason, I was too overwhelmed by the whole situation to even ask him his name. My world was just swirling around the coming baby and the anxiety of being alone through this whole ordeal.

We reached the hospital around two in the morning. The driver rang the bell of this little private maternity hospital. A nurse came out and escorted me in. He wished me good luck and left. I barely managed to thank him because by now my contractions were setting in.

At seven thirty-one, on January 29, 1982 Neptune was born and with this additional daughter, my life changed forever.

As I said earlier, over the years I have kept a journal of special moments with my daughters. This was written a few years after the girls were born.

"Dawn slips into day and day into dusk inevitably so will come adieus to explore the different shores of life and time.

My children were given to me as gifts for a long yet immensely short while.

Now these gifts have been worked upon, enhanced hopefully to catch the brilliance of the rainbow after the rain. They have been strengthened enough to know how to nurture a frail baby sparrow fallen from its nest on the windowsill and are wise enough to find enough earth to replant a tiny uprooted sapling.

They are silly enough to raise their heads to the sky and combat the light drizzle with their eyelids and catch a few delicious raindrops rushing maddeningly from the nose to the tip of the tongue.

Now I share every glance, every mood, and every tear. I share their very heartbeats.

As mother and daughters, we will grow apart. Their strong wings and dreams woven with neon lights in still dark nights will take them further than I can imagine.

Fusions of their dreams and mine are forever merging, entangling, dismantling, surfacing, hiding, traveling as lightly and yet unconditionally as stars kissing the ocean's face unknowingly. Conception somehow never ends. "

A few weeks after I got out of the hospital and was well I went to visit my angel driver. I learned that he no longer lived there. I did not know where he had moved. I tried to track him down but to no avail.

My daughters have always been a source of great joy and encouragement. They have been anchors, mentors and counselors. Above all they have always respected me and honored me as their mother.

A few years ago Neptune wrote me a beautiful song for Mother's day. I wish I could share the song with you but it is being copyrighted. She will perhaps add that to her own sweet seasons of miracles.

Neptune is now twenty-four and married to Derek, who is a wonderful person. She is studying to become a counselor.

In the still darkness of the night I needed a miracle and I found two.

One was the transportation to the hospital and the other the gift of a beautiful daughter.

*Notes*

_____

_____

_____

_____

_____

_____

_____

_____

_____

_____

_____

_____

_____

_____

_____

_____

_____

_____

_____

_____

_____

_____

_____

# Chapter - 30

## *The Miracle of a Daddy's Love*

It was just about five months since I was married and close to a year since I moved to the United States in July of 2002.

It was a bleak rainy day which is of course not unusual for the Northwest. What was unusual for me was to see about sixty or seventy homeless people lined up on a cold wintry day for some sandwiches and soup. The numbers had been increasing over the past few weeks.

A couple of times a week, I would network with the different feeding programs to see how I could help.

As I stood there shivering in the cold, I thought the winters here were really brutal. Having grown up near the equator where the temperature is 80 or 90 degrees year round, this was quite a drastic change.

I pulled my coat a little tighter, hoping to cut out the draft. Just then, I felt the Lord whisper to me, "Jewels, ask them where they get their meals every day."

I kind of suddenly suspected where this conversation was going. So I mustered all the courage I had and asked Ol' Bob, "Where do you get your meals every day, Bob?"

He began to name the different centers and churches that provided meals on the different days of the week. He mentioned all days except Monday.

Then I heard the Lord prompt me again and say, "Ask him why he missed mentioning Monday?"

"Bob," I said "Why did you miss Mondays?"

Bob looked at me kind of dejected and said, "There is no feed on Mondays."

Then this internal conversation with God kept going... "Jewels, tell him not to worry that you will be here next Monday by the bus station with a meal for everyone."

"God, you have got to be kidding. I am new here. I have no funds and well ...I am new here."

The Lord then asked, "Who provided for you when you were looking after all the street kids? Remember, I told you not to raise any funds or to look at man for provisions. Did I not provide, every single time you needed help?"

Remembering the past, sheepishly I said, "Yes Lord, what do you want me to do now?"

"Make an announcement that you will be here next Monday with lunch."

Over the years I had learned not to argue with God.

I raised my hand to get everybody's attention and said, "I have good news, next Monday I will be here with the lunch and probably every Monday after that."

Everyone cheered and clapped. Lunch having finished I drove home wondering what the future had in store.

I was new to this country. I did not have an organization to provide for this new venture. I shared the story with my husband Pete, and he willingly supported the feed.

Monday came and we made a whole bunch of sandwiches, packed some juice, some chips and started a soup kitchen right by the bus stand.

A few months later, the city police asked us not to meet near the bus stop to avoid congestion in the area.

Now I faced another challenge to overcome, another hurdle to cross. On talking with all my homeless friends they thought the park in the heart of the city would be a good place.

Summer was here and so it was a great time. We put a tarp on the grass, spread out the lunch, and had a wonderful time. Often we would share stories from our lives; our joys and sorrows, extending the mantle of God's love to whoever needed it.

Summer passed by quickly and then came fall and winter was round the corner. Each Monday the folks asked me where we were going to move when the rains came. I did not have an answer.

I did not know anybody in the city who would want to give me their church or some room or a basement. Practically no one knew me in the city.

In just a few weeks the rains would be here, and I was asked again, "Jewels, what are you going to do?"

"My Daddy's got to show up," I replied. I had no other plan.

Now I was really getting concerned, just one more week we would have trouble meeting out in the cold.

Andy, one of the young men who came to the meals said, "Jewels, it is going to rain next week, where are we going to meet?"

I looked at him smiled and said, "You know Andy I don't know anyone who would give me a place, my only hope is that my Daddy is going to show up."

A few minutes later, an elderly gentleman came and tapped me on the shoulder. He introduced himself as a Pastor of a local church which was situated just by the park.

He looked at me and asked, "What are you going to do next Monday? I hear its going to rain."

"Well," I said, "I believe my Daddy is going to show up before then."

He smiled and said, "Guess what? We have been praying for you, and now would like to offer you our basement to continue the work, not only during the rain but after that."

Next Monday it rained and Daddy had not only his daughter indoors but a whole bunch of his children whom He loves just as dearly.

Today, almost three years later the tiny little feeding program in the park has six or seven volunteers and sometimes more than fifty people show up for a single meal.

A new season has now begun in a new country with new people, new hope and new courage. A new season of miracles is taking wings, spurring me on to believe that God is able.

Wishing you God's best as you discover your own sweet seasons of miracles.

## Notes

_____
_____
_____
_____
_____
_____
_____
_____
_____
_____
_____
_____
_____
_____
_____
_____
_____
_____
_____
_____
_____
_____
_____
_____
_____

Dear Reader,

Hope this book was a source of inspiration to you.

I am sure that you have experienced wonderful miracles in your life time and would like to share them with others.

My goal is to publish another book, "Sweet Seasons of Miracles Around The World."

If you are interested in being part of the book please email me with a short story at author@sweetseasonsofmiracles.com.

Thank you and wishing you as always Sweet Seasons of Miracles.

Jewels Mesaros